The Natural History of Film Form

The Natural History of Film Form

Pansy Duncan

Edinburgh University Press is one of the leading university presses in the UK. Publishing new research in the arts and humanities, EUP connects people and ideas to inspire creative thinking, open new perspectives and shape the world we live in. For more information, visit www.edinburghuniversitypress.com.

© Pansy Duncan, 2025

Grateful acknowledgement is made to the sources listed in the List of Illustrations for permission to reproduce material previously published elsewhere. Every effort has been made to trace the copyright holders, but if any have been inadvertently overlooked, the publisher will be pleased to make the necessary arrangements at the first opportunity.

Edinburgh University Press Ltd
13 Infirmary Street, Edinburgh EH1 1LT

Typeset in 12/14 Arno and Myriad by
IDSUK (DataConnection) Ltd

A CIP record for this book is available from the British Library

ISBN 978 1 3995 4824 3 (hardback)
ISBN 978 1 3995 4825 0 (paperback)
ISBN 978 1 3995 4826 7 (webready PDF)
ISBN 978 1 3995 4827 4 (epub)

The right of Pansy Duncan to be identified as the author of this work has been asserted in accordance with the Copyright, Designs and Patents Act 1988, and the Copyright and Related Rights Regulations 2003 (SI No. 2498).

Contents

List of Figures vi
Acknowledgements vii

Introduction 1
1. Celluloid™: The Material Prehistory of the Plastic Image 24
2. Infected Gelatin and the Bacterial Life of Popular Science Cinema 49
3. Silver Salts and the Aesthetics of Early Studio-Era Hollywood Cinema 69
Conclusion: Lithium Aesthetics 97

Bibliography 103
Index 113

Figures

1.1 The opening frames of *Explosion of a Motor Car* hold out a promise of photographic realism (Cecil M. Hepworth, 1900). 37
1.2 The advent of the explosion recasts the image as a plastic object rather than a documentary record of the world (Cecil M. Hepworth, 1900). 39
1.3 The force of the blast opens the pro-filmic action into vertical space (Cecil M. Hepworth, 1900). 40
2.1 Jean Comandon's *Spirochaeta Pallida* (1909) depicts syphilis spirochetes as a series of fine, crinkled lines moving among large, luminous cellular bodies. 60
2.2 & 2.3 Included in an article published in *Transactions of the Society of Motion Picture Engineers* by two Eastman Kodak research scientists, these images show frames of motion picture film stock affected by mysterious markings that I contend were likely the result of bacterially infected gelatin. Source: Media History Digital Library. 61–62
3.1 *A Movie Trip Through Filmland* (Paul Fenton, 1921) favors shots of raw materials, like the bars of silver depicted here, over images of the workers who help process them. 78

Acknowledgments

I could not have begun this book, let alone completed it, without the support of the staff at the Margaret Herrick Library, the Eastman Library at the University of Rochester, the Bradford Museum of Science and Technology, and the British Film Institute, as well as the less visible but no less significant support of the people behind the Media History Digital Library. I owe them my deepest thanks. The financial backing of Massey University's SREF and, later, the Royal Society of New Zealand Te Aparangi, made these distant archives accessible. Thanks to the panellists of both the SREF and the Marsden Fund for their early faith in this project.

I am also indebted to the editors and anonymous reviewers at *Screen*, who gave the material that forms the basis of Chapter 3 its first outing. Further thanks are due to the many audiences who responded to early iterations of these chapters: colleagues and students in the film studies programmes at King's College, London, and the University of Otago, Dunedin, as well as participants in and organizers of the 2018 and 2020 Screen conferences, the 2019 SCMS conference and the 2022 Materials of Modernity conference.

Special thanks to William Brown and David Fleming for including this book in the Screens/Thinking/World series and for their thoughtful engagement with the manuscript. I am also deeply appreciative of EUP editors Gillian Leslie and Kelly O'Brien, who managed the review and production process with enthusiasm and efficiency.

This book is dedicated to Tim and Wolfie, who delight me every day.

Introduction

This short book argues that the raw or not-so-raw ingredients of early cellulose nitrate film stock—gelatin, celluloid, and silver—played a pivotal role in the evolution of early cinema's "radically heterogeneous" aesthetic practices.[1] The testimony of early filmgoers and filmmakers supports this argument. In the memoirs of cinema's directorial pioneers, we find scenes of stymied film production in which the "buckl[ing]" and "twist[ing]" of celluloid leads to prints that are "somewhat too substantial," or in which gelatin, "infected" with bacteria, leaves "little faint white spots" on the finished film text.[2] In early film criticism, meanwhile, we find these same ingredients suffusing spectatorial experience, from paeans to the "silver screen" to celebrations of cinema's unprecedented "plasticity."[3] Defying critical efforts to divide early cinema's rowdy bio- and geo-physical materials from its varied visual delights, these voices propose a direct, even formative, relationship between them. They suggest that, more than just feeding early cinematic technologies, the animal, vegetable, and mineral products of the modern extractive industries helped shape the perceived form and sensual experience of early cinema itself.

Existing critical literature is only beginning to provide purchase on this co-implication of "raw" materials and aesthetics. Within canonical film-historical scholarship, histories of early film aesthetics, and histories of early film technology's raw ingredients, tend to run on parallel tracks that rarely if ever intersect.[4] And emerging film-historical scholarship, perhaps most notably work appearing under the auspices of film history's so-called "materialist" and "eco-materialist" turns, is also unexpectedly limited in its affordances to this line of inquiry. On the one hand, newer "materialist" film scholarship—resisting Marxist film theory's tendency to mortgage "materialism" to political economy—has examined the constitutive effects of a range of material factors, from early studio architecture to early projection techniques, on cinema's evolving aesthetic regimes.[5] This body of literature is theoretically diverse, drawing, variously, from theories of the cinematic apparatus, film industries approaches, German media theory, and the so-called "new materialisms." It is unified, however, by a model of materiality that stays strictly at the macro-level of production and distribution hardware rather than scaling down to the micro-level of the organic ingredients feeding that hardware. As a result, critics associated with film history's materialist turn have barely entertained the possibility that ingredients like silver, celluloid, or gelatin might have played a role in shaping early cinema's aesthetic practices.

On the other hand, the influence of developments taking place in the field of media studies has seen the rise of "eco-materialist" approaches to film and film history.[6] In contrast to older "eco-critical" approaches that focus on cinematic representations of broader ecological phenomena, eco-materialist approaches have paid close attention to cinema's own ecological entanglements, from its implication in extractive capitalism to its legacies of environmental devastation.[7] In this context, the extraction, application, disposal, and circulation of film stock's raw ingredients are beginning to receive well-deserved and long-overdue attention.[8] It is now widely established, for example, that by 1920 the consumption of silver at Eastman Kodak—the principal supplier to Hollywood for much of the twentieth century—had reached three tons of silver bullion per week, far exceeding "any manufacturer of silverware" and rivaling that of the US mint.[9] Yet, with some important exceptions, this scholarship, like eco-materialist film scholarship more broadly, tends to pitch itself as part of a move away from the textual focus often associated with older eco-critical frameworks to a newer focus on production, industry, infrastructures, and environment.[10] One consequence of eco-materialist film scholarship's inattention to textual form is that scholars addressing film stock's raw materials have not explored the idea that these materials might have played a role in shaping cinema's aesthetic or audio-visual dimension. In fact, more often than not, scholars in the broader field of eco-materialist film and media studies scholarship subscribe to logics of demystification that represent media's visible, audible, and tangible surfaces as false fronts, "hiding," "concealing," or "disavowing" the web of connections to the natural environment that sustains them.[11] In an excellent reading of the use of water on the set of *Singin' in the Rain* (Kelly/Donen, 1952), for example, Hunter Vaughan impugns the finished film for its "disavowal" of the "hidden material consequences of production practices"; Robert Maxwell and Toby Miller identify their project as a means of "revealing" processes "hidden from us by fancy advertisements"; while Sean Cubitt's *Finite Media* contends that the visible dimensions of media "hide the truth of toxic media, the toxicity of production processes."[12] While it is now widely acknowledged, then, that film technologies, industries, and infrastructures relied on and continue to rely on what Jussi Parikka dubs "dirty matter," the field of film *aesthetics* remains surprisingly "clean."[13]

What neither materialist or eco-materialist approaches to film history consistently provides, then, is an account of how these raw biophysical and geological resources have left their "sediments and deposits" on media's visible, audible, and tangible register.[14] And in the case of eco-materialist accounts of film history, this oversight is underpinned by a pair of problematic assumptions about matter and matter's relationship to the aesthetic. The first is the assumption that early cinema's raw materials are essentially what Jane Bennett dubs "dead matter"—passive, inert substances that are instrumentalized by, but incapable of acting alongside, human endeavour.[15] The second—fed and facilitated by the first—is the assumption that film aesthetics exists in a spectral, metaphysical domain beyond matter, untouched by the raw materials, extractive processes, industrial infrastructures, and environmental harms that, by all accounts, sustain it. This dematerialized conception of the aesthetic is particularly limiting today. For scholars across the disciplines, it is now widely acknowledged that the human impact on Earth's ecosystems has been so profound that it has brought about a new geological epoch, variously conceptualized through the lenses of the Anthropocene, the Capitalocene, and the Cthulucene.[16] The new visibility of this epoch demands that we come to grips with the profound historical co-implication of nature and culture, of nonhuman matter and mass-mediated human creative practice.[17]

The Natural History of Film Form helps shed new light on this mutual entanglement by exploring the role of the key ingredients of nitrate film stock—gelatin, silver, and celluloid—in shaping early Euro-American film aesthetics. Thus, in Chapter 1, I consider the form of the trick film as an exercise in plasticity that is both prompted by, and reflects, the elastic and explosive possibilities of celluloid. In Chapter 2, I consider the possibility of a causal relationship between bacterially-infected gelatin and the "bacteria film" genre pioneered by French microbiologist Jean Comandon. In Chapter 3, similarly, I consider the extent to which the classical Hollywood cinema's status as what Lynn Festa calls a "sentimental commodity"—a status that accrues to a subset of commodities that purport to exist outside circuits of exchange—was fueled by the presence of silver in the stock during the early studio era.[18] As these summaries suggest, my focus is primarily on film as material object in the world rather than as disembodied figuration of the world. Thus, in a methodological departure from standard eco-critical approaches to the text, my argument is not that my chosen aesthetic configurations represent, thematize, or allegorize the bio and geo-physical ingredients that underpin them (although, as I will show, they sometimes do this too).[19] Rather, addressing the trick film, the popular science genre, and the cinema of early studio-era Hollywood, I show how popular aesthetic configurations that were "unable or unwilling" to register these raw materials directly nevertheless bear their insistent traces.[20]

In advancing this argument, I use the term "aesthetics" advisedly, with an eye to pushing beyond the limits often signaled by the term "form." As I will show below, a range of recent scholarship across the text-based disciplines—influenced, in part by a broader "turn to form" in literary and cultural studies—has examined the way in which textual forms reflect and respond to modern industrial resource economies.[21] However, its title notwithstanding, this book's argument is not simply that gelatin, silver, and celluloid helped mold early film form, but that they shaped early cinema's aesthetic configurations more broadly. In this, I follow Sianne Ngai in defining "aesthetics" as a category that encompasses both "the judgment[s] we utter, a way of speaking" and "the form[s] we perceive, a way of seeing—sutured by affect into a spontaneous experience."[22] Under the broad banner of film aesthetics, then, we can place a range of phenomena, from the form of objects, to the subjective feelings to which these forms give rise, to the category-based judgments into which these feelings often coalesce. Thus, in Chapter 3, I consider not just silver's role in driving the turn to classical Hollywood's narrative economies, but also its role in shaping widespread conceptions of Hollywood cinema as a mode infused by the magic of the so-called "silver screen." My argument about the influence of the bio- and geo-physical ingredients of film stock on film aesthetics, then, encompasses the claim that these materials shaped the subjective and social experience of early Euro-American popular cinema as well as the claim that they shaped its objective form.

With that said, the filmic image remains central to any account of film aesthetics, and thus my effort to track the multi-scalar connections between materials and aesthetics depends, in part, on a re-conceptualization of that image. In this respect, it should come as no surprise that models of the image that emphasize its materiality, from German media theory to more recent work in visual culture studies, are touchstones for this book.[23] As W. J. T. Mitchell has reminded us, in a sweeping account of the mass-mediated image, if "an image is a sign or symbol of something by virtue of its sensuous resemblance to what it represents," it cannot "*merely* signify or represent something."[24] Rather, the image is also, irreducibly, "a material object," by which Mitchell appears to mean that it is technologically mediated.[25] However, as I have already suggested, accounts of the materiality of the image that conflate "materiality" with "media technology" are not entirely adequate to the task of mapping the relation between gelatin, silver, and celluloid and early Euro-American film-aesthetic regimes. For there are important differences in scale, form, and structure between, say, a media technology (such as a strip of film stock) and the silver crystals that are dispersed invisibly and in microscopic quantities through the filmic emulsion. In this regard, Giuliana Bruno's account of materialism's implications for the image, which favors the term "surface" over the term "image," proves salutary for my analysis. According to Bruno, "the visual text is fundamentally textural. . . . It is made out of layers and tissues. It contains strata, sediments, and deposits. It is constituted as an imprint, which always leaves behind a trace."[26] This conception of the image—as a surface composed of layered substances that inevitably bear traces of their formation—offers a way of mapping the more haphazard and aleatory routes through which, the early Euro-American cinematic image received the "imprint" of the raw materials of nitrate film stock.

While emphasizing the need for further work addressing this convergence between the raw materials of film stock and early film aesthetics, I don't wish to underplay the profound debt this book owes to existing eco-materialist film histories that have sought to explore other material interfaces between film aesthetics and the natural environment, as well as the extractive industries that mediate these interfaces. Though not focusing in a sustained way on the ingredients of film stock, film scholars James Leo Cahill, Jennifer Fay, Brian Jacobson, and Elena Past, for example, have produced brilliantly illuminating scholarship in this space. In *Inhospitable World*, Fay traces points of contact between the environmental world-building at play in the Anthropocene, and the creative world-building at play in the process of film production, showing, for example, how the "experiments in manufactured weather" that took place on the sets of Buster Keaton movies "tap into an interwar awareness that 'natural' disasters were often attributable to industry and war," and thus that "nature" was already bound up with culture.[27] Similarly, Cahill's 2019 article, "Cinema's Natural History," shows how film texts can be read as historically-situated negotiations between the constructed and the discovered, between artificial and natural ecosystems, thus troubling both their distance and their distinction from the natural resources that sustain them.[28] Finally, Past's *Italian Ecocinema: Beyond the Human* reinscribes signature features of Italian neorealism—the long take, the handheld camera, the use of nonprofessional actors—as evidence of neorealist productions' intense relationships to the places in which they were set and shot.[29]

Perhaps the book that dovetails most closely with this one is Brian Jacobson's *The Cinema of Extraction*, which, like my own, seeks to bridge what he identifies as a "gap" between "textual" approaches and "contextual" studies of industry, materiality, technology, and environments.[30] By way of doing so, Jacobson calls for "a return to formalism" that is attuned to the processes by which both the raw materials powering filmmaking technology, and the extractive industries devoted to procuring them, become visible on-screen.[31] Despite overlap between our broader respective agendas, Jacobson's book diverges in significant ways from this one. First, Jacobson does not address the raw materials of nitrate film stock, although, alongside the carbon and tungsten used for theatre projectors and studio lights, he does explore petroleum (a central ingredient of later acetate-based stocks). Second, the forces he identifies as an overlooked formal factor in shaping his chosen texts are less the materials *per se* than the resource industries that worked to extract them. Finally, his textual focus is on films that are, as he puts it, either "explicitly about extraction or . . . engage[d] with extractive content": industrial and corporate films that depict extraction directly; feature films and documentaries that take extractive industries as their subject; and what he terms a "cinema of 'resource extraction,'" in which extraction functions as a "structuring absence."[32] While he does explore the extent to which logics of extraction "impress[ed]" themselves on his chosen films' "form," representation necessarily remains a key element of his attempts to fold together the textual and the contextual.[33] By contrast, my focus is on ways in which commercial films that are not explicitly about the materials that sustain them, from the trick film to popular "bacteria" film of the 1910s, nevertheless remain "touched" by these materials at the aesthetic register. Despite these differences between our respective projects, there remain important convergences between them, especially in their shared effort to integrate modes of analysis that are often kept unnecessarily apart.

Beyond film studies, scholarship inflected by the environmental humanities in the adjacent fields of art history and literary studies have also proved salutary for this book, modeling ways of reading texts for traces of the resource economies that shape and sustain them. Frederick Buell has shown how the nineteenth- and twentieth-century shift from coal-based capitalism to oil capitalism gave rise to "a new, exuberant rhetoric that rejects the very notion of stability and equilibrium and that celebrates risk and even imminent catastrophe as part of this new dynamism."[34] Amanda Boetzkes has contended that petroculture "conditions vision" through a logic of plasticity that is central to the practices of contemporary artists Portia Munson, Song Dong, Melanie Smith, and Choi Jeong-Hwa.[35] Stephanie LeMenager writes of the role of oil in structuring the book as a material object. As LeMenager reminds us, "the ink that creates the words on the page"—"words that direct [the] imagination and activate [the] senses"—is "largely a mixture of petroleum-based resins and oil."[36] Finally, Nathan K. Hensley and Philip Steer, drawing on a broader turn to form across literary studies, identify what they call "coal form" as a point of affinity between the otherwise very different novels of Elizabeth Gaskell, J. R. Seeley and Joseph Conrad, tracing this distinctive form to the coal-powered energy systems that comprised the Victorian novel's common condition of possibility.[37] While the bulk of environmentally-minded scholarship in the text-based disciplines focuses on the way texts represent or intervene in global resource economies, Buell, Boetzke, LeMenager, Hensley, and Steer show how texts are moulded by features of these same economies. In this respect, they fulfill Sheena Wilson, Imre Szeman, and Adam Carson's call to attend to the extent to which natural resources "shap[e] our existence close at hand while narrating us into networks of power and commerce far, far away."[38]

Scope, Methods, and Methodology

As its length suggests, *The Natural History of Film Form* is modest in its scope. This is reflected in its narrow geographic and industrial focus, which takes in elements of the cinematic output of the early British, French, and US industries, but leaves out the very different outputs of, say, early Japanese, Australian, or Soviet industries. (One justification for this narrow focus on the US-UK-France is the fact that the industries of these three countries were, for much of the period this book covers, the most prolific in terms of production capacity and the most prominent in terms of reach and influence.[39]) The book's circumscribed scope is also manifest in its approach. Rather than aspiring to comprehensive coverage, even of the handful of industries in its purview, the book focuses on a trio of emblematic scenes that fall between the years 1900 and 1930. These case studies, I argue, illuminate significant moments of intersection between the early cinema's eco-material base and its shifting aesthetic regimes. In Chapter 1, for example, I connect pioneering English filmmaker Cecil M. Hepworth's experiments with the so-called "trick film," and his emerging sense of the "plasticity" of the image, to his documented encounters with the elasticity and explosiveness of celluloid. In Chapter 2, I explore the extent to which the widespread disavowal of gelatin's ongoing status as animal matter underpins the surprising *lack* of convergence between the early "bacteria film" and gelatin emulsion's vulnerability to infection. In Chapter 3, I consider the distinct profile of silver as a sentimental commodity alongside 1920s fan-journal paeans to the wonders of the "silver screen." Drawing heavily from original archival research at the Eastman library (Rochester), the Margaret Herrick Library (Los Angeles), the National Science and Media Museum (Bradford), the BFI (London), and the Media History Digital Library (online), I apply close textual analysis to the historical materials I have found in order to draw out both manifest and encrypted meanings; close analyses of filmic material, however, will be limited.

At a theoretical level, this textual analysis is informed by a synthesis of new materialist and Marxist accounts of matter. To address the former framework first, this project's emphasis on the role of silver, gelatin, and celluloid in shaping film aesthetics clearly involves ascribing to these materials a greater quantum of "agency" than is usually attributed to them; in this sense, it bears obvious debts to what has become known as the "new materialism," an interdisciplinary body of inquiry that insists on what Stacy Alaimo calls "the agency and significance of matter."[40] Of course, the specific visions of matter that have anchored new materialist approaches diverge—from Jane Bennett's work on material objects as performative agents in political life, to Brian Massumi and Eve Sedgwick's work on the affective dimension of the body, to the philosophical work of theorists Ian Bogost and Graham Harman on the ontology of the "stuff" that populates late consumer capitalism.[41] Yet scholarship associated with the so-called new materialism converges on a commitment to exploring material and/or embodied realities beyond their discursive inscriptions while challenging conventional views of matter as either an inert, passive substance or as a socially constructed fact. In their place, a model of materiality as excess, force, vitality, relationality, or difference has come to the fore. From a new materialist perspective, there is little difference between older film scholarship's treatment of the ingredients of motion picture stock as a quiescent supplement to the motion picture industry's representational agendas and the newer eco-materialist scholarship's treatment of the same ingredients as an egregiously exploited supplement to that same agenda. Both reduce matter to a purely instrumental role within human aesthetic, ideological, and industrial enterprises. By contrast, this book emphasizes matter's power to confound these same enterprises, installing a nonhuman element at the heart of the cinematic apparatus in ways that complicate persistent claims about cinema's status as a distinctly "human" medium.

However, while my account of the *agency* of these materials is consistent with the tenets of new materialism, my account of the *nature* of these materials is heavily indebted to Marxist reflection on the role of capitalist social relations in shaping the form and application of the object-world.[42] Resisting new materialism's reification of matter, the book is animated by the assumption that the supposedly neutral geo- and biophysical constituents of early film technology are always already embedded within specific historical relationships of production, consumption, and distribution, which shapes them at both a physical and imaginative level. As Alice Lovejoy notes of film stock, "politics are . . . embedded in the 'support' itself— in its raw materials, industrial processes and circulation."[43] It is in order to account for the "embedded[ness]" of the political in the materiality of stock that I will refer to silver, celluloid, and gelatin as "politico-material" rather than simply "material" objects.[44] In this respect, two registers of the political will be particularly prominent here. The first relates to these ingredients' implication in socially binding practices of extraction, production, circulation, consumption, and disposal. As I argue in Chapter 1, for example, celluloid's flexibility and malleability at once crystallized the promise of modern production processes and came to emblematize some of its threats.[45] However, I also pay close attention to the racialization of these materials, for accounts of celluloid's "plasticity" are inextricably bound up with fantasies of the black(ened) body. Not only is plasticity central to popular conceptions of Blackness, but the large-scale cultivation and circulation of cotton, one of the primary constituents of celluloid, is rooted in the transatlantic history of slavery. The racialized aspect of the politico-material profile of celluloid is key to the aesthetic imaginary of the early trick films that combustible celluloid helped to shape. Similar observations animate the other two chapters of the book, which treat gelatin, silver, and celluloid as uniquely modern fusions of "natural" and "human" history.[46]

Regardless of these equivocations, an argument yoking film aesthetics to film's "raw materials" entails a somewhat mechanistic causal logic that must be acknowledged and accounted for. Film studies scholars have long expressed skepticism about causal narratives in general, and "mechanistic" causal narratives in particular.[47] In *Reading Capital*, Louis Althusser, whose structuralist approach to Marxism has been foundational to film studies, argues that a mechanistic model "reduce[s] causality to a transitive and analytical effectivity, [and can]not be made to think the effectivity of a whole on its elements, except at the cost of extraordinary distortions."[48] According to Althusser, this form of causality is both overly deterministic ("transitive") and overly focused on the causal role of extrinsic factors at the expense of factors that are "immanent in [their] effects."[49] Yet, for Fredric Jameson, mechanistic models of causality have a more complicated status in radical Marxist praxis. On the one hand, as Jameson notes, it is difficult to draw clear distinctions between a mechanistic model of causality and models that are central to a more reputable Marxist tradition, such as the base/superstructure framework, for example, which also involves a certain mechanistic determinism. On the other, even assuming we could draw such clear distinctions,

> It does little good. ... to banish 'extrinsic' categories from our thinking, when the latter continue to have a hold on the objective realities about which we plan to think. There seems, for instance, to have been an unquestionable causal relationship between the admittedly extrinsic fact of the crisis in late nineteenth-century publishing, during which the dominant three decker lending library novel was replaced by a cheaper one-volume format, and the modification of the 'inner form' of the novel itself. The resultant transformation of the novelistic production of a writer such as Gissing must thus necessarily be mystified by attempts of literary scholars to interpret the new form in terms of personal evolution or of the internal dynamics of purely formal change ... what is scandalous is not this way of thinking about a given formal change, but rather the objective event itself, the very nature of cultural change in a world in which separation of use value from exchange value generates discontinuities of precisely this 'scandalous' and extrinsic type.[50]

Here, Jameson seeks to redeem mechanical causality on the basis that, if used carefully, it can register the "scandalous" logic of a social arrangement in which aesthetic questions are overly dependent on the contingencies of the "material base of cultural production."[51] It is this "scandalous" logic to which I hope this book draws attention. While often understood in idealist terms as a "mirror" or "expression" of the society in which it exists, film aesthetics is also a mass-produced industrial product of that society. Like other such products—from soap to shoes—its warp and woof is textured by the mode, form, and ingredients of the industrial processes in which it is caught up.

It is worth offering two further points of clarification about the nature of the agency this book attributes to silver, celluloid, and gelatin, respectively. First, I do not wish to suggest that these specific materials were the only—or even the most important—material forces shaping early cinema's evolving aesthetic regimes. Rather, more modestly, I hope to show that they must be numbered among the host of different agencies that shaped the aesthetic practices I describe, from changes in the structure of the industry, to the rise of new exhibition sites and shifts in audience demographics.[52] The work of these other agencies is reflected in the fact that, while the composition of film stock after 1900 was relatively standardized globally, films outside the US-UK-France axis were nevertheless delivering very different cinematic forms, from early Soviet montage to German Expressionism and early Japanese recordings of *kabuki* or *shinpa* plays, often accompanied by a *benshi* narrator.[53] Thus, this book's argument about the role of cellulose, gelatin, and silver seeks to complement rather than replace existing accounts of the evolution of early film aesthetics. A second point of clarification about the agency of these raw materials is that the efficacy of this agency will vary somewhat across the course of the book. In some cases, these raw ingredients will function as what Bruno Latour calls "mediators," in the sense that they directly "transform, translate, and distort" the systems in which they are caught up.[54] For example, as I will show in the second half of the third chapter, the sharp uptick in silver prices following World War I directly affected the shape of the early classical style, with efforts to avoid wasted stock helping mandate the rise of Hollywood's sleek, standardized aesthetic economies. In other cases, however, I describe silver as what Latour calls an "intermediary," "transport[ing] meaning or force without transformation" and an instrument (if a crucial one) in an agenda that pre-existed it and exceeded it in scope. For example, as I will show in the first section of the same chapter, Hollywood's PR machinery routinely exploited the supposed magic of the silver content in film stock in order to sustain popular fantasies of the magic of the silver screen.[55]

As this suggests, the phrase "natural history" in my title carries significant weight. Unlike the organisms that are the traditional object of natural history as a domain of scientific inquiry, film form and the feelings and judgments that congeal around it are a product of human artifice. Yet, I insist, they are not *only* a product of human artifice, and, by mobilizing the phrase "natural history," I reposition film aesthetics as a product both of bio- and geo-physical processes and of human activity. In so doing, I am inspired by posthumanist challenges to human exceptionalism that emphasize the entanglement of human and nonhuman agencies, the co-constitution of species and technologies, and the critique of anthropocentric boundaries.[56] However, I am also inspired by the substantial tradition of critical commentary that Cahill unpacks in his essay "Cinema's Natural History." According to Cahill, while generally referring to the study of living organisms in their natural environment, for figures like Theodor W. Adorno, Walter Benjamin, and Siegfried Kracauer, "natural history as a mode of looking at and interpreting the world's signs" involves an estranging and inherently "surrealist" gaze, challenging the anthropocentrism that assimilates film history to human history by emphasizing the contingency, materiality, and fragility of the former.[57] My hope is that this book can engender something of the aesthetic and theoretical estrangement that Benjamin and Adorno mobilized the figure of "natural history" to invoke, enabling us to look freshly at a practice in which natural resources and human endeavor combine in the production of what Fay calls cinema's "artificial worlds."[58]

Chapter Summaries

The opening chapter of this book, "Celluloid™: the Material Prehistory of the Plastic Image," implicates the primitive thermoplastic, celluloid (which served as the base for early photosensitive emulsions), in an aesthetic development crucial to cinema's early period. In doing so, it first sets out celluloid's peculiar "politico-material" profile. In particular, it shows how this heavily industrialized vegetable derivative, synthesized from cellulose and treated with nitrate, emerged at once as an ideally pliant, flexible ingredient that served to crystallize the promise of modern production processes, *and* as a dangerous, explosive substance that came to emblematize some of the dangers associated with those same processes. Then, turning to a case study of pioneering English filmmaker Cecil M. Hepworth, it shows how celluloid's unique politico-material properties helped mediate Hepworth's turn from an exclusively photographic conception of the cinematic image (which emphasized its status as a record of a prefigured reality) toward an understanding of the "plastic" possibilities of the cinematic image (which recognized its capacity for manipulation, transformation, and illusionism). Through close analysis of both Hepworth's early film writings and his early film output, it argues that the director's burgeoning appreciation of film's plastic as opposed to its purely photographic affordances, and his concomitant turn to the trick film, was routed in part through a series of encounters with the conflicting potentials of this "pioneer plastic."[59]

In the second chapter, "Infected Gelatin and the Bacterial Life of Popular Science Cinema," I explore the relation between film stock gelatin's vulnerability to bacterial infection and the "bacteria" film—an early scientific form of visualization in which bacteria played a prominent role. By way of doing so, I first outline gelatin's politico-material status in the early cinematic period, arguing that, at this point in history, gelatin was understood neither as an animal derivative nor as entirely not-animal, but rather as "animal no more"—its animal connections relegated to the past in a gesture that disavowed what scientists today understand is its ongoing susceptibility to the standard vicissitudes of animal matter, including bacterial infection. Having established this, I will go on to set side-by-side two texts, both of which emerged in the period 1909–1919, and both of which deal with bacteria in some form. The first is a 1909 "bacteria film" by French microbiologist and filmmaker Jean Comandon entitled

Spirochaeta Pallida, showing syphilis spirochetes (the spiral-shaped bacteria that cause syphilis) shimmying and jerking across the cornea of an eye. The second, produced a few years later, is a series of still images by Kodak emulsion scientists J. I. V. Crabtree and G. E. Matthews showing raw film stock marked by a series of mysterious spots at which Crabtree and Matthews express confusion, but which are readable today as the result of bacterially infected gelatin. These two texts are not obviously linked. On the contrary, significant aesthetic differences between the two suggest that the vicissitudes of the gelatin content of motion picture film stock failed to register explicitly in the practice of bacteria film. Yet, as I will show, the very non-coincidence of these two texts attests to the force of gelatin's politico-material profile as a substance whose constitution as "animal no more" made the ongoing effects of gelatin's animal origins illegible.

My third chapter zeroes in on the silver content of film stock to advance an argument about its role in shaping Hollywood film aesthetics in the early "classical" period (the decade or so immediately following World War I [1918–1930]). First, it briefly revisits a range of existing scholarship on the classical Hollywood cinema in an effort to ground the claim that the "classical Hollywood style" was essentially a commodity aesthetic that combined a fetishistic or "magical" allure with standardized narrative and formal economies. Then, it draws on original research across a wide variety of archival sources to intervene in debates about why this contradictory commodity aesthetic gained the stylistic dominance it did. More specifically, it contends that, thanks to its dual politico-material profile as both a "sentimental commodity" and a "money commodity," silver also played a role in shaping the classical Hollywood cinema's contradictory aesthetic character.[60] As a "sentimental commodity" that embodied what Karl Marx describes as the commodity's "magic" force, silver helped support the discourses of film "magic" by which the classical Hollywood cinema of the 1920s laid claim to a mystical transcendence of market logic.[61] And as what Marx calls a "money commodity," silver played a part in fostering these same cinematic practices' all too visible *adherence to* the logic of the market, helping shape the rise of classical Hollywood narrative economies.[62]

Across each of these three chapters, I seek to situate early cinema's signature aesthetic practices in relation to the fickle geo- and biophysical ingredients of early film stock. Yet as I show in my conclusion, "Lithium Aesthetics," these links between cinema's eco-material and aesthetic registers do not expire with the obsolescence of film stock. Similar exchanges can be traced in the context of film shot, distributed, and projected using digital technology, with lithium's logic of speed, efficiency, and lightness arguably providing ballast for the new cinema of speed. Mapping these exchanges between aesthetics and materials is vital. It is vital if we are to develop a fuller historical picture of the evolution of film aesthetics. It is vital if we are to do better theoretical justice to modern technological media's imbrication in the natural world. And it is vital if we are to design more effective methodological tools for tracing the relationship between a set of unprecedentedly industrialized aesthetic practices and an ornery, never-entirely-industrialized natural world.

Notes

1. Jennifer M. Bean, "Introduction," in *A Feminist Reader in Early Cinema*, eds. Jennifer M. Bean and Diane Negra (Durham, NC: Duke University Press, 2002), 6.
2. Frederick A. Talbot, *Moving Pictures: How They Are Made and Worked* (London: William Heinemann, 1914), 25; Cecil M. Hepworth, *Came the Dawn: Memories of a Film Pioneer* (London: Phoenix House, 1951), 79.
3. For vernacular references to the "silver screen," see Advertisement, *Motion Pictures News*, April 22, 1922, 2268; Advertisement, *Photoplay Magazine*, February 1928, 125; Anonymous, "Production Highlights," *Exhibitors' Trade Review* 33, no. 8 (April 25, 1925). For the use of the rubric of plasticity by early film critics, see Sergei Eisenstein, *Eisenstein on Disney*, ed. Jay Leyda, trans. Alan Upchurch (London: Methuen, 1988), 21; Élie Faure, "Cineplasticity," in *Film: An Anthology*, ed. Daniel Talbot (Berkeley, CA: University of California Press, 1966), 6.
4. Thus, on the one hand, we find historians of early film aesthetics, whose nuanced descriptions of the evolution of its "varied visual delights" tend to ascribe them to the cultural, social, and technological transformations of industrial modernity. For foundational examples of this work, see Leo

Charney and Vanessa R. Schwartz, *Cinema and the Invention of Modern Life* (Berkeley: University of California Press, 1995); Anne Friedberg, *Window Shopping: Cinema and the Postmodern* (Berkeley: University of California Press, 1994); Tom Gunning, "The Cinema of Attractions: Early Film, its Spectators and the Avant-Garde," in Wanda Strauven, ed., *Cinema of Attractions Reloaded*, 381–388 (Amsterdam: Amsterdam University Press, 2005); Tom Gunning, "An Aesthetic of Astonishment: Early Film and the (In)credulous Spectator," *Art and Text* 34 (Spring 1989): 31–45; Miriam Hansen, *Babel and Babylon* (Cambridge, MA: Harvard University Press, 2009). On the other, we find historians of early film technology, many of whom are attentive to the often-unruly animal, vegetable, and mineral derivatives that fed early photographic film stock but who have little investment in drawing links to specific aesthetic practices. See, for example, Michael Chanan, *The Dream that Kicks: The Prehistory and Early Years of the Cinema in Britain* (London: Routledge, 1996), 68–77; Leo Enticknap, *Moving Image Technology* (New York: Wallflower Press, 2005); Deac Rossell, *Living Pictures* (Albany, NY: State University of New York Press, 1998); Anthony Slide, *Nitrate Won't Wait: A History of Film Preservation in the United States* (Jefferson, NC: McFarland, 2013); Roger B. N. Smither, *This Film Is Dangerous: A Celebration of Nitrate Film* (Brussels: Federation Internationale des Archives du Film [FIAF], 2002).

5. For just a few examples of this scholarship, see Sheri Biesen, *Blackout: World War II and the Origins of Film Noir* (Baltimore: JHU Press, 2005), 63; Brian R. Jacobson, *Studios Before the System: Architecture, Technology, and the Emergence of Cinematic Space* (New York: Columbia University Press, 2015); Jocelyn Szczepaniak-Gillece and Stephen Groening, "Afterword: Objects in the Theater," *Film History* 28, no. 3 (2016): 139–142; and the essays collected in a special issue of *Recherches Semiotiques/Semiotic Inquiry* 31, nos. 1/2/3 (2011), entitled "Cinéma & Technologie"/"Cinema & Technology."

6. The growing body of eco-materialist literature on film includes Nadia Bozak, *The Cinematic Footprint: Lights, Camera, Natural Resources* (New Jersey: Rutgers University Press, 2012); Priya Jaikumar and Lee Grieveson, eds., "Film and Extraction," special issue, *Media+ Environment* 6, no. 1 (2024); Nicole Shukin, *Animal Capital: Rendering Life in Biopolitical Times* (Minneapolis: Minnesota University Press, 2009); Hunter Vaughan, "500,000 Kilowatts of Stardust," *Sustainable Media*, eds. Janet Walker and Nicole Starosielski, 23–37 (New York, NY: Routledge, 2016); Hunter Vaughan, *Hollywood's Dirtiest Secret: The Hidden Environmental Costs of the Movies* (New York: Columbia University Press, 2019). This literature is influenced by and shaped by approaches in media studies more broadly, including, for example, Sean Cubitt, *Finite Media: Environmental Implications of Digital Technologies* (Durham, NC: Duke University Press, 2016); Richard Maxwell and Toby

Miller, *Greening the Media* (Oxford: Oxford University Press, 2011); Jussi Parikka, *A Geology of Media* (Minneapolis, MN: University of Minnesota Press, 2015); Janet Walker and Nicole Starosielski, *Sustainable Media* (New York, NY: Routledge, 2016).

7. For just a few examples of this more traditional eco-critical approach to cinema, see Alexa Weik von Mossner, *Moving Environments: Affect, Emotion, Ecology, and Film* (Waterloo, ON: Wilfrid Laurier University Press, 2014); Sean Cubitt, Stephen Rust, and Salma Monani, *The Ecocinema Reader: Theory and Practice* (New York: Routledge, 2012); Selmin Kara, "Anthropocenema: Cinema in the Age of Mass Extinction," in *Post-Cinema: Theorizing 21st Century Film*, eds. Shane Denson and Julia Leyda (Sussex, UK: Reframe, 2016), 750–784; Joseph K. Heumann and Robin L. Murray, *Ecology and Popular Film: Cinema on the Edge* (Albany: State University of New York Press, 2009); David Ingram, *Green Screen: Environmentalism and Hollywood Cinema* (Exeter, UK: University of Exeter Press, 2004); Brian R. Jacobson, "*Ex Machina* in the Garden," *Film Quarterly* 69, no. 4 (Summer 2016): 23–34; Paula Willoquet-Maricondi, ed., *Framing the World: Explorations in Ecocriticism and Film* (Charlottesville: University of Virginia Press, 2010); Pietari Kääpä and Tommy Gustafsson, *Transnational Ecocinema: Film Culture in an Era of Ecological Transformation* (Chicago: Intellect, 2013); E. Ann Kaplan, *Climate Trauma: Foreseeing the Future in Dystopian Film and Fiction* (New Brunswick, NJ: Rutgers University Press, 2015). The eco-materialist focus on the material sources and impacts of cinema is usually represented as part of an effort to move "away from issues of film representation" that dominated older eco-critical frameworks in favour of attention to "the geopolitics, industrial infrastructure, and material impact of media industries and practices" (Vaughan, *Hollywood's Dirtiest Secret*, 10).

8. See, for example, Alice Lovejoy, *Tales of Militant Chemistry: The Film Factory in a Century of War* (Berkeley, CA: University of California Press, 2025); Shukin, *Animal Capital*; Benjamín Schultz-Figueroa, "From Cattle to Beef Onscreen: Animal Rendering as Extraction in Industrial Livestock Films," *Media+ Environment* 6, no. 1 (2024); Emmet von Stackelberg, "'The Fatal Blemish': Purity, Consistency, and Chemical Engineers at the Origin of a New Visual Order, 1890–1930," *Enterprise & Society* (2024): 1–26. For related work in the adjacent field of the history of photography, see Siobhan Angus, *Camera Geologica: An Elemental History of Photography* (Durham, NC: Duke University Press, 2024).

9. Lee Grieveson, *Cinema and the Wealth of Nations: Media, Capital, and the Liberal World System* (Berkeley: University of California Press, 2018); Alice Lovejoy, "Celluloid Geopolitics: Film Stock and the War Economy, 1939–47," *Screen* 60, no. 2 (2019): 224–241; Maxwell and Miller, *Greening the Media*. For contemporary accounts, see H. E. Gausman, "More Silver

Used in Films than in Coins," *The Film Daily* 9 (March 6, 1927); Kodak Historical Collection, Department of Rare Books, Special Collections and Preservations, University of Rochester River Campus Libraries, Rochester, NY (hereafter KHC), box 39, folder 11, "A Kind of Magic," 26.

10. These "important exceptions" include Lovejoy, *Tales of Militant Chemistry* and Brian Jacobson, *The Cinema of Extractions: Film Materials and Their Forms* (New York: Columbia University Press, 2025). See also Hunter Vaughan, "The Fifth Element: Hollywood as an Invasive Species and the Human Side of Environmental Media," in *Hollywood's Dirtiest Secret* (New York: Columbia University Press, 2017), 20; and Jonathan Haid, "The Raw Materials of Celluloid Film: Wartime Economy, Educational Animation, and Film's Plasticity," in *Research in Film and History* 5 (2023): https://film-history.org/issues/text/raw-materials-celluloid-film

11. Admittedly, some recent eco-materialist scholarship has sought to heal this conceptual rift between film's eco-material and aesthetic registers, attending to the damage wrought to specific film texts by the decay of the nitrocellulose film base, as film's "seething surface" is progressively "raddled by time" (Cubitt, *Finite Media*, 5; Amy Herzog, "Assemblage, Constellation, Image: Reading Filmic Matter," *Discourse* 38, no. 2 [2016]: 6). While compelling, however, these accounts focus less on the formative scene of film production than on the *post hoc* scene of archival decay, as if cinema's raw materials only acquire formative powers when they begin to droop and ossify. *A Natural History of Film Form* also diverges significantly in its aims from scholarship on the role of film stock's raw materials in the context of artisanal, experimental, and avant-garde film practices. Exemplary volumes that touch on this topic include Kim Knowles, *Experimental Film and Photochemical Practices* (New York: Spinger, 2020), Gregory Zinman, *Making Images Move: Handmade Cinema and the Other Arts* (Berkeley, CA: University of California Press, 2020) and Scott MacKenzie and Janine Marchessault, eds., *Process Cinema: Handmade Film in the Digital Age* (Ontatio: McGill-Queen's, 2019). In contrast to these books, my own book addresses the role of raw materials in shaping popular cinematic practice.

12. Vaughan, "500,000 Kilowatts," 35; Maxwell and Miller, *Greening the Media*, 22; Cubitt, *Finite Media*, 110.

13. Jussi Parikka, "New Materialism as Media Theory: Medianatures and Dirty Matter," *Communication and Critical/Cultural Studies* 9, no. 1 (2012): 95–100.

14. Giuliana Bruno, *Surface: Matters of Aesthetics, Materiality, and Media* (Chicago: University of Chicago Press, 2014), 5.

15. Jane Bennett, *Vibrant Matter: A Political Ecology of Things* (Durham, NC: Duke University Press, 2010).

16. Christophe Bonneuil and Jean-Baptiste Fressoz, *The Shock of the Anthropocene: The Earth, History and Us* (London: Verso Books, 2016); Jeremy Davies, *The Birth of the Anthropocene* (Berkeley: University of California Press,

2016); Donna Haraway, "Anthropocene, Capitalocene, Plantationocene, Chthulucene: Making Kin," *Environmental humanities* 6, no. 1 (2015): 159–165; Jason W. Moore, "The Capitalocene, Part I: On the Nature and Origins of Our Ecological Crisis," *The Journal of Peasant Studies* 44, no. 3 (2017): 594–630.
17. Jussi Parikka, *Digital Contagions: A Media Archaeology of Computer Viruses* (New York: Peter Lang, 2007).
18. Lynn Festa, *Sentimental Figures of Empire in Eighteenth-Century Britain and France* (Baltimore, MA: Johns Hopkins University Press, 2006), 115.
19. For some examples of this body of work, see endnote 7 in this chapter.
20. Nathan K. Hensley and Philip Steer, "Signatures of the Carboniferus: the Literary Forms of Coal," in *Ecological Form: System and Aesthetics in the Age of Empire*, eds. Nathan K. Hensley and Philip Steer (New York: Fordham University Press, 2019).
21. For examples of this broader turn to form, see Caroline Levine, *Form: Whole, Rhythm, Network* (Princeton: Princeton University Press, 2015); Marjorie Levinson, "What Is New Formalism?", *PMLA* 122, no. 2 (2007): 558–569; Franco Moretti, *Atlas of the European Novel: 1800–1900* (London: Verso, 1999).
22. Sianne Ngai, *Theory of the Gimmick: Aesthetic Judgment and Capitalist Form* (Cambridge, MA: Harvard University Press, 2020), 1.
23. Friedrich A. Kittler, *Gramophone, Film, Typewriter* (Stanford, CA: Stanford University Press, 1999); Bernard Siegert, *Cultural Techniques: Grids, Filters, Doors, and Other Articulations of the Real*, trans. Gregory Winthrop-Young (New York: Fordham University Press, 2015).
24. W. J. T. Mitchell, "Image," in *Critical Terms for Media Studies*, eds. W. J. T. Mitchell and Mark B. N. Hansen (Chicago, IL: University of Chicago Press, 1985), 30.
25. Mitchell, "Image," 39.
26. Bruno, *Surface*, 5.
27. Jennifer Fay, *Inhospitable World: Cinema in the Time of the Anthropocene* (Oxford: Oxford University Press, 2018), 18.
28. James Leo Cahill, "Cinema's Natural History," *Journal of Cinema and Media Studies* 58, no. 2 (2019): 152–157.
29. Elena Past, *Italian Ecocinema: Beyond the Human* (Bloomington: Indiana University Press, 2019).
30. Jacobson, *Cinema of Extractions*, 6.
31. Jacobson, *Cinema of Extractions*, 8.
32. Jacobson, *Cinema of Extractions*, 16, 21.
33. Jacobson, *Cinema of Extractions*, 16.
34. Frederick Buell, "A Short History of Oil Cultures: Or, the Marriage of Catastrophe and Exuberance," *Journal of American Studies* 46, no. 2 (2012): 279.

35. Amanda Boetzkes, "Plastic Vision and the Sight of Petroculture," in *Petrocultures: Oil, Politics, Culture*, eds. Sheena Wilson, Adam Carlson, and Imre Szeman (McGill-Queen's Press-MQUP, 2017), 222–41.
36. Stephanie LeMenager, "The Aesthetics of Petroleum, after Oil!" *American Literary History* 24, no. 1 (2012): 64.
37. Hensley and Steer, "Signatures of the Carboniferus."
38. Sheena Wilson, Imre Szeman, and Adam Carlson, "On Petrocultures: Or, Why We Need to Understand Oil to Understand Everything Else," in *Petrocultures: Oil, Politics, Culture*, eds. Sheena Wilson, Adam Carlson, and Imre Szeman, 1–19 (Montreal: McGill-Queen's Press, 2017), 1.
39. Richard Abel, *The Ciné Goes to Town: French Cinema, 1896–1914* (Berkeley, CA: University of California Press, 1998); Kristin Thompson and David Bordwell, *Film History: An Introduction* (New York: McGraw-Hill Education, 2003); Rachel Low, *The History of the British Film 1906–1914* (London: Routledge, 1997).
40. Stacy Alaimo, *Exposed: Environmental Politics and Pleasure in Posthuman Times* (Minneapolis: Minnesota University Press, 2016), 1. Karen Barad, *Meeting the Universe Halfway: Quantum Physics and the Entanglement of Matter and Meaning* (Durham, NC: Duke University Press, 2007); Jane Bennett, *Vibrant Matter: A Political Ecology of Things* (Durham NC: Duke University Press, 2012).
41. Brian Massumi, *Parables for the Virtual: Movement, Affect, Sensation* (Durham, NC: Duke University Press, 2021); Eve Kosofsky Sedgwick, *Touching Feeling: Affect, Pedagogy, Performativity* (Durham, NC: Duke University Press, 2003); Ian Bogost, *Alien Phenomenology, or, What It's Like to Be a Thing* (Minneapolis: University of Minnesota Press, 2012); Graham Harman, *Object-Oriented Ontology: A New Theory of Everything* (London: Penguin UK, 2018).
42. Karl Marx, *Capital: Critique of Political Economy, Volume 1* (London: Penguin, 2024).
43. Lovejoy, "Celluloid Geopolitics," 224–5.
44. Bill Brown, "Materiality," in *Critical Terms for Media Studies*, eds. W. J. T. Mitchell and Mark B. N. Hansen (Chicago: University of Chicago Press, 2010), 59–60.
45. Jeffrey L. Meikle, *American Plastic: A Cultural History* (New Brunswick: Rutgers University Press, 1995).
46. Dipesh Chakrabarty, "The Climate of History: Four Theses," *Critical Inquiry* 35, no. 2 (2009): 197–222.
47. Thomas Elsaesser, "The New Film History as Media Archaeology," *Cinémas* 14, no. 2–3 (2004): 76, DOI: https://doi.org/10.7202/026005ar

48. Louis Althusser, Etienne Balibar, Roger Establet, Pierre Machery, and Jacques Ranciere, *Reading Capital*, trans. Ben Brewster and David Bernbach (London: Verso, 2016), 186.
49. Althusser, et al., *Reading Capital*, 189.
50. Fredric Jameson, *The Political Unconscious: Narrative as a Socially Symbolic Act* (New York: Routledge, 1983), 10.
51. Jameson, *The Political Unconscious*, 10.
52. David Bordwell, Janet Staiger, and Kristin Thompson, *The Classical Hollywood Cinema: Film Style and Mode of Production to 1960* (New York: Routledge, 2003); Douglas Gomery, *Shared Pleasures: A History of Movie Presentation in the United States* (Madison: University of Wisconsin Press, 1992).
53. For the latter, see Aaron Gerow, "Early Cinema: Difference, Definition and Japanese Film Studies," in *The Japanese Cinema Book*, eds. Alastair Phillips and Hideaki Fujiki (London: Bloomsbury, 2020), 25.
54. Bruno Latour, *Reassembling the Social: An Introduction to Actor-Network Theory* (Oxford: Oxford University Press, 2007), 39.
55. Latour, *Reassembling the Social*, 39.
56. Rosi Braidotti, *The Posthuman* (Malden, MA: Polity Press, 2013); Haraway, "Anthropocene, Capitalocene, Plantationocene, Chthulucene"; Cary Wolfe, *What Is Posthumanism?* (Minneapolis: University of Minnesota Press, 2010).
57. Cahill, "Cinema's Natural History," 153.
58. Fay, *Inhospitable World*, 9.
59. Robert Friedel, *Pioneer Plastic: The Making and Selling of Celluloid* (Madison: University of Wisconsin Press, 1983).
60. Douglas Gomery, *The Hollywood Studio System: A History* (London: Bloomsbury Academic, 2005); Tom Gunning, "Modernity and Cinema: a Culture of Shocks and Flows," in *Cinema and Modernity*, ed. Murray Pomerance (New Jersey: Rutgers University Press, 2005), 297–315; Janet Wasko, *Movies and Money: Financing the American Film Industry* (Stamford, CT: ABLEX Publishing Corporation, 1982).
61. Karl Marx, *Capital: A Critique of Political Economy, Vol. I* (London: Penguin, 2004), 169.
62. Michael Heinrich, *An Introduction to the Three Volumes of Karl Marx's Capital* (New York: NYU Press, 2012), 67.

Chapter One

Celluloid™: The Material Prehistory of the Plastic Image

I.

In the June 4, 1897 edition of his weekly column for British journal *The Amateur Photographer*, pioneering English filmmaker Cecil M. Hepworth—then better known for his work in magic lantern than in motion picture projection—described an encounter with a trick screening involving a piece of filmed footage being "run through the machine backwards."[1] When projected as normal, he notes, the screening is "but 'the usual thing' in animated photography."[2] Yet when the footage is played in reverse, the brief dramatic episode featuring an intoxicated gentleman's "return home after dining well" takes a turn for the "astonishing":

> His braces fling themselves over his shoulder ... his waistcoat flies from the floor and adjusts itself in position ... and then the gentleman backs out of the room in a very peculiar manner, after having given the most curious performance in topsyturvydom that has ever been dreamed of since the days of 'Alice Through the Looking-Glass.'[3]

On the face of it, the incident related by this column entry is unremarkable. By 1897, screenings featuring the reversal of footage were an "established attraction," and anecdotes tracing the waves of spectatorial awe or horror that greeted these performances litter the historical record.[4] What is striking about Hepworth's take on this microgenre, however, is the two forms of "plasticity" it conjures. Hepworth's reference to "the view ... run through the machine backwards" calls attention to the early vegetable-derived thermoplastic, celluloid, that served as photographic film stock's transparent, flexible support and that provides the material basis for the "extraordinary" aesthetic effects Hepworth goes on to chronicle.[5] And Hepworth's reference to the screening's aesthetic effects as a "curious performance in topsyturvydom" evokes the aesthetic rubric of "plasticity" that, by the end of the nineteenth century, dominated emerging efforts to capture the cinematic image's transformative and metamorphic rather than merely photographic possibilities (these efforts are exemplified by C. Francis Jenkins' reference to motion pictures as one of the "most plastic of all forms of energy," and by W. K. L. and Antonia Dickson's celebration of their capacity to bring "all the kingdoms of the world . . . into the plastic scope of individual requirement").[6] The two registers of "plasticity" at play in Hepworth's anecdote, the material and the aesthetic, are not unrelated. On the one hand, the "plastic" aesthetic quality of the image on screen prompts Hepworth to turn his attention to the celluloid running in reverse through the projector. On the other, the manipulation of the celluloid is the material precondition of the "plastic" aesthetic effects described.

What would it mean to probe the moment of contact that Hepworth's column stages—contact between the literal plastic that serves as the base of photographic film stock and an emerging metaphorics of the cinematic image that took "plasticity" as its lodestar? What would it mean, in particular, to explore this interface in relation to Hepworth's own evolving understandings of the aesthetic capacities of the medium? The material significance of celluloid in the development of early motion pictures as a technological apparatus is by now well-established, thanks to both classic technical histories and newer eco-materialist histories of the medium.[7] Yet the anecdote above suggests that, *as* a constituent of cinema's technological register, celluloid also touches cinema's aesthetic register—where the aesthetic is understood, with Sianne Ngai, as both the realm of "objective" textual properties, like form and genre, and as the realm of "subjective, feeling-based judgments" about them.[8] Certainly, we would not want to underplay the extent to which the rubric of "plasticity" is indebted historically to the classical paradigm of the "plastic arts" and thus, etymologically speaking, to the Greek *plassein*, which means "to model" or "to mould."[9] This classical rubric far predates, and indeed lent its name to, the class of compounds that came to be known as "plastics." Yet as design historian Jeffrey Meikle argues, by the end of the nineteenth century, the quality of plasticity was tightly yoked to the early thermoplastic known as "celluloid" and famed for its pliancy, resiliency, and flexibility. In fact, so tightly yoked was it that the term "plasticity" tended more immediately to call forth this novel industrially-produced material than the classical discourse from which the material received its name.[10] It is no accident, I suggest, that among early twentieth-century commentators seeking to capture cinema's capacity for transformation, metamorphosis and artifice, it was the trademarked term "celluloid" that enjoyed immediate popular uptake. As this suggests, what Élie Faure calls cinema's singular "cineplasticity" was closely laminated to celluloid itself.[11]

This chapter teases out this insight by implicating celluloid, a literal plastic, in Hepworth's early evolution from a realist or photographic conception of the cinematic image toward a more manipulable and "plastic" conception of the image. In advancing this argument, I will first set out the peculiar "politico-material" profile of this heavily industrialized vegetable derivative. In particular, I will show how celluloid, synthesized from cellulose and treated with nitrate, emerged at once as an ideally pliant, flexible ingredient that served to crystallize the promise of modern production processes, and as a dangerous, explosive ingredient that came to emblematize some of the dangers associated with those same processes. I will also explore how these antinomies were racialized as a result of plasticity's association with black(ened) bodies. Then, turning to Hepworth, I will show how, alongside the industrial, economic, environmental, and cultural factors that have been documented in detail by other scholars, celluloid's unique properties helped mediate his changing aesthetic agenda. Through close analysis of both his early film writings and his early film output, I will argue that the director's emerging appreciation of film's plastic as opposed to its purely photographic affordances, and his concomitant turn to the trick film, was routed in part through a series of encounters with the conflicting potentials of this early thermoplastic. In advancing this argument, I aim to make two primary interventions. First, I seek to complicate our understanding of the history of film aesthetics by tracing key elements of early cinematic form not, as is conventionally the case, to cultural, industrial, or technological developments, but to the unpredictable social, economic, discursive, and material agency of celluloid. Second, I hope to extend eco-materialist film histories by revealing the unexpected significance of celluloid, one of its conventional objects of study, to genealogies of film aesthetics.

II.

When first made available for commercial use as a flexible base for filmic emulsions in 1889, celluloid had a well-established politico-material profile that tied it both to the new possibilities of modern industrial production methods, and to the risks associated with those same methods. On the one hand, the material first manufactured as Parkesine (1856) and as Xylonite (1869), before being registered as *Celluloid* in 1870, was immediately celebrated for its capacity to transform, to imitate, and to substitute. Indeed, its "ability to assume many degrees of shape, texture, hardness, density, resilience or color" saw it quickly put to use in the mass production of a diverse array of goods.[12] By 1880, the Celluloid Manufacturing Company had issued licenses for its use by almost two dozen other firms, which engaged in the manufacture of celluloid dental plates, harness trimmings, dishes, knife and cutlery handles, emery wheels, combs, brushes, stays, shirt cuffs and collars, shoes, piano keys, watercolor cases, and a variety of jewelry items and fancy goods in imitation pearl, coral, amber, marble, and mosaic, as well as the more practical syringes, grinding wheels, or linings for ice pitchers.[13] As the copy on one of the Celluloid Manufacturing Co.'s 1878 advertising circulars had it, "like the fabled Proteus," celluloid could, once "rendered plastic by heat," be "molded into any desirable form," and take on "any desirable shade."[14] This transformative potential is built into its name: the suffix "-oid" is from the Greek *-oeidēs*, meaning equivalent to or derivative of, so that celluloid means, quite literally, "like cellulose." This framing doesn't just install simulation at the very heart of celluloid, but casts celluloid as a simulation *of itself*. In fact, so plastic and flexible was celluloid that it served to substantiate claims about the plasticity and flexibility of the modern production processes that gave rise to it. In celluloid, that is, swiftly-industrializing Western countries found compelling evidence of the capacity of new modes of production to "make anything out of anything," "transform[ing objects] rapidly before one's eyes" with a "speed ... [that] made it appear magical."[15] And the relationship between industrial modernity's powerful mechanisms of production and this, its paradigmatic product, was reciprocal. As Meikle has noted, while the natural limits of wood, stone, and metals "made it hard to conceive of material desires beyond the traditional ... that situation changed ... when chemists learned to synthesise substances that had never before existed and to specify their properties."[16] In other words, celluloid's shape-shifting qualities opened up the possibility of a world of manufacturing that exceeded traditional "needs" and spilled into the realm of fantasy.

Yet if celluloid's peculiar plasticity both came both to embody and to shape the promise of modern industrial production, it also emblematized some of its perils. When the Hyatt brothers had first tried to interest manufacturers of hard rubber goods in their substitute material, one manufacturer rebuffed them on the basis that they were likely to blow themselves up.[17] And these fears were quickly borne out in practice. An 1874 editorial in the *New York Times*, "Explosive Teeth," describes cases of combustive dental work exploding in wearers' mouths; the April 1882 issue of *Scientific American* reports that the celluloid buttons on the "dress of a lady, standing near a bright fire, had one of the buttons of her dress ignited"; and an 1893 issue of the same journal chronicles a dramatic case of exploding celluloid-backed toilet brushes, ignited through proximity to a "hot air register."[18] Realistically, the cases documented by the news items above were rather unusual. Yet the attention they drew in the popular press reminds us that, as Catherine Malabou has put it, plasticity's power to give and receive form has as its flipside the power to destroy and annihilate form—as suggested, Malabou proposes, by the use of "the term 'plastic' explosive for a bomb."[19] It also points to a more general skepticism about the modern manufacturing methods that celluloid had come to represent. If modern industrial production methods delivered a cornucopia of new commodities, they also delivered a host of new anxieties about identity and class in a nascent consumer culture that had dislodged traditional means of establishing and measuring social position.[20] And there was no better object lesson in industrial modernity's broken promises than the tendency of one of its crowning commodities, celluloid, to blow up in the user's face.

Accounts of "plasticity," moreover, are complexly racialized in ways that deepen our understanding of the fundamental antinomies of celluloid's political-material profile. On the one hand, ideas of plasticity are key to theoretical conceptions of White, Western modernity: for Karl Marx, industrial capitalist modernity famously sees "all that is solid melt into air," while for Zygmunt Bauman, modernity itself is "liquid."[21] On the other, plasticity is key to theoretical conceptions of the role of Blackness in modernity. Thus, for Anna Arabindan-Kesson, in modernity, "Blackness flickers back and forth, unfixed and malleable, like a raw material always in the process of being refined," while for Zakiyyah Iman Jackson, dominant visions of Blackness are shaped by narratives of plasticity in which Black(ened) bodies emerge as "infinitely malleable lexical and biological matter, a plastic upon which projects of [both] humanization *and* animalization rest."[22] Moreover, the extraction and production of the ingredients feeding celluloid further racialize this material. Recall, for example, that one of the primary ingredients in nitrocellulose, itself a core component of celluloid, was cotton; that, at the turn of the century, Kodak, one of Cecil M. Hepworth's primary suppliers of raw stock,[23] obtained its celluloid from the Celluloid Company, a leading manufacturer of the material; and that the Celluloid Company, in turn, sourced cotton primarily from the

American South—a connection that evokes the history of slavery and the plantation economy, along with the Black laborers whose lives were inextricably bound to it. As Arabindan-Kesson observes, cotton is "a site where Blackness is elided and yet most graphically brought to life."[24]

By the time celluloid was adapted for use as a base for gelatin emulsions, then, it came complete with a number of baked-in potentials, both material and political, both desirable and disruptive, and bound up with both White and Black modernity. But how, exactly, might the politico-material properties of the distinctive compound have helped shape Hepworth's early apprehension of the cinematic image? Before answering this question, it is worth tracing, in very broad strokes, the contours of his early aesthetic programme—a programme that underwent a radical transformation in the space of a few short years. The son of author and lanternist T. C. Hepworth, Hepworth junior spent his early life in a whirl of "photography-limelight-lantern shows-lectures" and had become involved with Birt Acres in the very early days of filmmaking, assisting Acres at a Royal film performance at Marlborough House.[25] Yet despite his training as a showman, Hepworth's earliest films, produced during his brief tenure as a director for Charles Urban's Warwick Trading Company, speak to a conception of filmmaking as "a passive act" primarily involving the "record[ing of] reality."[26] The same is true of Hepworth's earliest feature for his own company, Hepworth and Co., established very soon after Urban let him go. According to a surviving catalog that includes a range of films made across the company's first year of production, 1899, these initial titles are almost entirely actualities or topicals, while the occasional fiction films, most of them turning on comic incidents, do not employ trick techniques.[27] Yet if Hepworth's very earliest work conformed quite readily to a conception of the cinematic image as a reflection of a prefigured reality, by 1900, Hepworth had gone on to produce some of the most notorious trick films of the early period. These include *Explosion of a Motor Car* (Hepworth and Co., 1900), in which, after the titular explosion of a motor car, the body parts of the driver and passengers fall from the sky, and

Clown and Policeman (Hepworth and Co., 1900), in which a clown blows a policeman to pieces before reassembling him. Deploying an array of innovative production and post-production devices, from explosion effects to substitution splices, these films index a model of the cinematic image as a "plastic" or moldable object rather than as a visual document.

Hepworth's oscillation between realist and "plastic" apprehensions of the moving image was not at all unusual in an incipient film culture that was in no way a coherent or integrated network of visual theories and practices. On the one hand, early "animated views" were celebrated for their photographic capacity to provide a pure record of time and movement, and linked referentially, whether through indexical or iconic models of signification, to the world beyond. Manifesting in a flurry of popular commercial pictures that French illusionist and director Georges Méliès called "natural views" or "scientific views," this early, documentary conception of the moving image has been the subject of a range of recent scholarly commentary.[28] On the other, moving images were just as routinely celebrated for their plastic capacities—their capacity "to conjure a world of fantasy" through the modification of real-time recording.[29] Perhaps best reflected in the trick film or *vue à transformations*, with their logics of magical transformation, and later, in stop-motion, drawn or painted animation, this conception of the cinematic image cast live action footage, where it was used at all, as "raw material" that could be crafted in ways that, as Tom Gunning has put it, were "unconfined by the forms of actuality."[30] Certainly, the observation that early popular film culture was under the sway of two primary, competing understandings of the cinematic image risks falling afoul of now-classic critiques of "the Manichean division between the films of Lumière (documentary; realism) and the films of Méliès (fiction; fantasy; stylization)."[31] These critiques emphasize the powerful similarities *across* early filmmaking practices, whether at the level of their shared mode of address, as in Gunning's account of early cinema's performative, presentationalist logic, or at the level of their shared assumptions about the nature of the spectator, as in Jonathan Crary's argument about the "corporeality of the observer."[32] Yet to admit that early films shared a single mode of appeal or a single set of assumptions about the observer is not to rule out the existence of distinctions in style and content between "the realistic illusion of motion offered to the first audiences by Lumière" and "the magical illusion of motion concocted by Méliès."[33] On high popular rotation at the time, these distinctions remain in critical circulation today.[34]

There is ample evidence that, in Hepworth's case, at least, celluloid helped mediate the transition from "realist" to "fantastical" models of cinematic illusion. Certainly, the distinctive qualities of celluloid would not have been lost on Hepworth, who had been at least as heavily involved in film development and film printing as in film production processes since well before joining the Warwick Trading Company in 1897.[35] And in his 1897 volume, *Animated Photography: the ABC of the Cinematograph*—a short filmmaking handbook published just prior to his directorial debut at Warwick—this changing vision of the cinematic image can be quite decisively routed through a series of encounters with the ingredient. Across its first few pages, the handbook elides celluloid's materiality altogether, idealizing its status as an aid or auxiliary to the "photograph" that rests upon it. In the course of a description of some of the earliest innovations in motion picture technology, for example, Hepworth announces, upon reaching the early 1890s, that "the next remarkable achievement was the Edison kinetoscope," which enabled "really satisfactory photographs upon a flexible support [to] be produced by the aid of *transparent celluloid*."[36] From Bela Balázs through Siegfried Kracauer and André Bazin, the figure of "transparency" has been central to realist theories of the cinematic image that cast the apparatus as an "incorporeal intermediary between observer and world."[37] Hepworth's emphasis on "transparent celluloid," then, serves to propagate these abiding fantasies of the "primal transparency of the camera obscura."[38]

Yet if the opening pages of *Animated Photography* represent celluloid as a "transparent," infra-thin surface, later pages register its full material force—doing so, at least initially, in powerfully positive terms that are reminiscent of the Celluloid Manufacturing

Company's paeans to the wonders of celluloid's manipulability, flexibility, and plasticity. Returning to Edison, for example, Hepworth notes that "By the use of celluloid ... he was able to produce an almost incredible number [of pictures] in a given space of time, and to continue to produce them at a rate until there were enough to record a complete little episode"—an anecdote that casts celluloid less as a passive, transparent vehicle for light-sensitive photographic emulsions than as an active representational accelerant.[39] Yet, in keeping with celluloid's ambivalent logic as a material that is both infinitely flexible and potentially explosive, no sooner has it acquired material status than it begins to assume other, less pliant and predictable forms—providing, in the process, the basis for a thoroughly novel reconceptualization of the image. This new, plastic vision of the cinematic image initially emerges in the course of Hepworth's account of early film-editing practice. According to this account, prior to the use of montage, editing was generally less a matter of assembling a range of shots into a single scene than of "stringing [a range of one-shot] pictures together into little sets or episodes" for exhibition purposes—a process to which celluloid's plasticity was integral.[40] Indeed, as Leo Enticknap explains, it was celluloid's plasticity that made it possible to cut lengths of film supplied by manufacturers and to join them together in different configurations.[41] Yet, for Hepworth, the material's plasticity doesn't just enable him to synthesize existing, naturalistic depictions of the world, but opens up new, plastic possibilities for the image itself. As Hepworth warns the reader, one should

> cut the film *before* joining it, that the picture or space in which the join occurs shall be a whole picture's breadth; otherwise, when the second animated photograph comes to be projected on the screen, it will be found to be displaced with respect to the mask of the instrument, and probably the photograph will appear cut in half and the halves transposed. To see the people in the picture bisected at the waist and their legs walking about on their heads may be a grotesque sight, but it is not pretty or desirable.[42]

"Bisected at the waist," their "legs walking about on their heads," the figures represented in this accidental conjugation of two separate images are an uncanny prefiguration of those "impossible bodies" that, according to Tom Gunning, would routinely be delivered by the trick film's "fascination with the construction and metamorphosis of the image."[43] They also recall William Brown and David Fleming's analogy between cinema and the cephalopod, which underscores cinema's "connecting and connected tentacles, and its shape-shifting simulating form."[44] What is important for our purposes, however, is the role that celluloid plays in mediating this evocation of a newly plastic image. The same plasticity that allows two pieces of celluloid to be joined and amalgamated according to the filmmaker's whim also allows them to be mis-amalgamated and mis-joined, conjuring "impossible bodies" that have no equivalents in or claim to a referential relationship to the world, and that, as such, anticipate the trick film's ability to "manipulate the exact rendition of the visual impression that an actual scene would provide to an eye-witness."[45]

This is not the only point in the handbook at which the evocation of the plasticity of celluloid prompts Hepworth to posit a more "plastic" model of the cinematic image. Yet the volume's later mentions of celluloid show the material's "explosive plasticity" at its more treacherous extremes—reminding us that an emphasis on the plasticity of the image can point us beyond the manipulation of the image's referential promise to an abandonment of that referential promise altogether. Exemplary here is a chapter entitled "Precautions Against Danger," in which Hepworth details the role of celluloid in the notorious Bazar de la Charité fire of 1897. According to Hepworth, the cause of the "horrible catastrophe that befell the unfortunates at a Parisian bazaar in the spring of the present year" was not the cinematograph itself, but the paraphernalia with which it is associated—including "the mass of very inflammable celluloid which is [often] allowed to accumulate in a basket or box or on the floor."[46] Neither a transparent aid to vision, nor an alternately ductile and defiant plastic, celluloid emerges from this meditation as an amorphous, baggy "mass" that, "accumulate[d] in a basket or box or on the floor," lacks form altogether. As such, celluloid finds its ultimate expression in what Isobel Armstrong calls the "formlessness of fire"—and serves as a literalization of Peter Szendy's and Akira Lippit's analogies between cinema and incineration ("To *cinefy*," Lippit concludes, is both "to make move, to make cinema and to incinerate, to reduce to ashes").[47] At stake here, again, is the ambivalent status of a plasticity that, for Malabou, just as readily describes "the destruction and the very annihilation of all form" as it does "the crystallization of form and the concretization of shape."[48] While lending itself to crafting, shaping, and manipulation, celluloid's plasticity also lends itself to defacement and destruction, so that, far from preserving or recording the object-world, it reduces the object-world to dust and ash.

In implicating celluloid in Hepworth's transition from a photographic to a plastic account of the cinematic image, it would not do, of course, to elide the other influences that would have shaped this account. In the early Warwick catalogs, Hepworth's "own-brand" actualities for Warwick sat cheek-by-jowl alongside trick and fantasy films imported from France and produced by Méliès' Star Films, while in his weekly column for *The Amateur Photographer*, Hepworth was referencing trick effects as early as June 1897, in his account of "cinema extraordinary."[49] Indeed, as a host of critics have shown, the trick film's debts are multivarious. They range from so-called "pre-cinematic" devices like serial photography and magic lantern projections to the other pictorial and projection practices—stage magic shows, *féeries*, quick-change, *tableaux vivants*, "chapeaugraphy" and shadowgraphy—that competed alongside film for the new, late nineteenth-century leisure dollar.[50] In this respect, it is worth noting that magic lantern projections, Hepworth's own speciality prior to his embrace of motion pictures, also deployed trick techniques, as in the "trick slides" of what Hepworth calls the "*Sleeping Man Swallowing Rat* description."[51] Yet while Hepworth's knowledge of other pictorial traditions is undeniable, evidence also points to the role of a material more specific to the filmic medium in shaping his growing appreciation of film's plastic potentials: celluloid.

In fact, this relation between the combustible plasticity of celluloid on the one hand and an emergent conception of the cinematic image as a "plastic" image on the other is reflected in Hepworth's earliest trick films. For a remarkably high proportion of Hepworth's "trick" output relies on the spectacle of the explosion—a spectacle that, as Hepworth himself admitted in 1897, was tightly "bracket[ed]" to celluloid.[52] Of his first four trick films, which were released in his second year as the operator of an independent production outfit, three feature scenarios of explosive disassembly or explosive transformation.[53] The most famous of these was also his very first, July 1900's *Explosion of a Motor Car*, which uses stop-motion, substitution-splicing techniques to show a motor car exploding skyward and its pieces plummeting back to earth.[54] But there is also the now-lost *The Gunpowder Plot*, a "gag" film that was released slightly later the same month, and that, according to a 1903 Hepworth catalog, involves a mischievous boy setting a "formidable Chinese cracker" under the chair of an elderly gentleman, and blowing him to smithereens.[55] Finally, there is *Clown and Policeman*, a mischief gag/chase film hybrid in which the antics of an unruly clown, a tramp, and a policeman are strung together to license the use of a number of similar tricks, one of which sees the policeman explode (before being put back together). Close analysis of these films suggests that this repeated conjugation of trick edit and celluloid-esque explosion is no mere coincidence—thus helping install scenes of "explosive plasticity" at the very origin of the plastic model of the image embodied in the trick edit.

Exemplary here is the first and perhaps most famous of the trio, *Explosion of a Motor Car*, a comic short whose sales "were the biggest we had had up till then."[56] As the film opens, a car containing three passengers draws toward the fixed camera, advancing from background to mid-ground, at which point it spontaneously explodes. Amidst the puff and perturbation, pieces of human and vehicular debris—a dismembered leg, a severed head, and a broken fender—are propelled out of frame, only to fall back into frame, piece by piece, at the feet of a passing policeman, whose conscientious efforts to document the falling wreckage are the comic focus of the final frames. At the heart of the film's appeal, then, are two "special effects," one involving pyrotechnics and the other a combination of stop-motion and substitution splicing (aka the "trick edit"). And while existing accounts of the relationship between early cinematic pyrotechnic effects and trick edits have tended to grant the latter historical priority, figuring the explosion as a means of masking or obscuring the cut, *Explosion of a Motor Car* troubles and even inverts

Figure 1.1 The opening frames of *Explosion of a Motor Car* hold out a promise of photographic realism (Cecil M. Hepworth, 1900).

this view.[57] The conflagration of an automobile, after all, is quite literally the film's headline spectacle. From this perspective, far from the explosion serving as a supplement to the trick edit, the trick edit serves as a supplement to the explosion. Certainly, a later film in Hepworth's July 1900 trio of trick films, *Clown and Policeman*, puts paid to the former hypothesis; three of the four trick edits in that film take place without (need for) accompanying smoky distractions. Treating the explosion as a proxy for celluloid, then, it is possible to argue that *Explosion of a Motor Car* positions celluloid at the origin of the "plastic" conception of the moving image epitomized by trick editing practices like substitution-splicing and stop-motion.

The narrative logic of *Explosion of a Motor Car* further substantiates this relationship between the explosive event and a plastic model of the image. For the advent of the explosion, at the film's mid-point, inaugurates a decisive stylistic break from a realist mode to a trick film mode that points, again, to a "plastic" vision of the image. As Figure 1.1 shows, the film's opening frames promise to "set [the filmed object] before us . . . in time and space" in the sort of miraculous "transference of reality from the thing to the reproduction" celebrated by André Bazin.[58] Among these frames' manifold markers of "realism" are the setting—a dusty suburban street appropriate to the actuality or "street scene" genre; the appearance of various, seemingly random, passersby in the background, who embody the logic of "singularity and contingency" that, according to Mary Ann Doane, has helped substantiate the moving image's claims to indexicality; and the depth of field showcased by the movement of the car through space, from deep background to mid-foreground—where depth of field was one of Bazin's favored mechanisms for guaranteeing realism by underscoring the continuity and duration of dramatic space.[59] As this suggests, while the opening frames of the majority of early comic shorts serve to foreshadow the climactic moment through suspense-building "preparatory action[s]" (a boy steps on a hose; a maid tries to light the stove), the opening frames of *Explosion* set the scene for a quite different kind of film.[60] And it is the sudden explosion of the car halfway through the film that serves to mark this stylistic transition—turning the everyday street-scene into a marvel of airborne mortal and mechanical debris, and replacing photographic realism with fantasy and stylization (see Figure 1.2). The (celluloid-esque) explosion, in other words, institutes a gear-shift in our relation to the cinematic image, transfiguring it from a record of a prefigured world into a moldable and plastic object.

Indeed, in its one-and-a-half-minute duration, *Explosion* provides a baked-in explanation for the radical stylistic transformation ushered in by the explosion spectacle—by underscoring the radical spatial transformation that is inherent to the explosion. As the film makes all too clear, the explosion involves a radical shake-up of standard spatial and temporal logics: spatially, it entails both fragmentation into a series of smaller pieces and expansion into a single colossal event, and temporally, it is both punctual and protracted, at once over in a single moment and ramifying into the future.[61] While, prior to the explosion, the events in *Explosion* take place on the horizontal or terrestrial plane, the force of the blast opens the pro-filmic action into what Kristin Whissel calls "vertical space," propelling the

Figure 1.2 The advent of the explosion recasts the image as a plastic object rather than a documentary record of the world (Cecil M. Hepworth, 1900).

fragments of the exploded vehicle into the area above the frame, from which they descend, one by one, back into the shot (see Figure 1.3).[62] As this suggests, the stylistic shift set in motion by the film's climactic pyrotechnic spectacle is bound up with the physics of the explosion itself. For the explosion's spatial and temporal contradictions push up against the limits of a cinematic practice understood as a matter of "recording" or "documenting" the world.[63] Successfully visualizing the explosion's "explosive plasticity" demands recourse to the plastic manipulation of the visual technology used to shoot it—that is, to some kind of in-camera or post-production wizardry. To recast this according to the allegorical logic that identifies the explosion spectacle with combustible celluloid, we might say that, in order to capture the logic of celluloid, Hepworth was forced to conceptualize the cinematic image in the novel, "plastic" terms embodied by the trick edit.

Figure 1.3 The force of the blast opens the pro-filmic action into vertical space (Cecil M. Hepworth, 1900).

The "plastic" model of the image mandated by the challenge of combustible celluloid is even more clearly in evidence in *Clown and Policeman*, which utilizes not one but a series of trick edits. In many explosion-oriented trick films produced around this time, the central conflagration serves as a narrative terminus, whether of a comic or grotesque kind (see, for example, *The Finish of Bridget McKeen* [Edwin S. Porter, 1901], *The Finish of Michael Casey* [Edwin S. Porter, 1901], *They Found the Leak* [AMB, 1902]). Yet, riffing on what Gunning calls "the theme of the disassembled and reassembled body," *Clown and Policeman* exploits the explosion's capacity not only to disassemble the body, but to provide the occasion for its full re-assembly—and thus, it would seem, for further plastic manipulation of the image.[64] The film's climactic explosion takes place when the titular policeman, unaware that the criminal duo he has been chasing have lit the fuse on a barrel of gunpowder, sits himself down on the barrel, leading to what Gunning dubs the mischief gag's "explosive payoff."⁶⁵ As the smoke clears, we see the policeman's headless body lying athwart a pile of rubbish. The effect of a trick edit, in which the image of the actor playing the policeman has been replaced by the image of a series of disparate body parts, this substitution is partially obscured by the diffuse shapelessness of the accompanying smoke. Yet the explosion does not mark the end of the action. Instead, the "plastic" model of the image established by the explosion precipitates further experiments with trick editing technique—a technique set loose, now, from its explosive origins. The next trick effect takes place in the wake of efforts by the clown and his sidekick to reassemble the policeman's dismembered corpse (the tramp propping him upright while the clown pops his head back on his shoulders); no sooner have they put him back together than there is a flash of light, and, in the third trick edit, the policeman has come back to life, only to recommence his pursuit. The final trick edit takes place when the revitalized policeman finally grabs hold of the clown—only for the latter to evacuate his oversized costume through a simple substitution-splice, leaving the policemen holding empty cloth. In its proliferation of trick edits, *Clown and Policeman* suggests that, once summoned by the spectacle of flammable celluloid, a "plastic" model of the image diffuses itself across the body of the film.

Another early Hepworth "gag" film, *The Gunpowder Plot* (1900), not only offers a further lens on the role of combustible celluloid in shaping the emergence of the trick film, but ties this process to celluloid's racialization. Indeed, a contemporary catalog description of the short explains that the explosion that forms the film's dramatic centerpiece is set off by a "Chinese" firework—a detail that implies the role of non-Whiteness in the key events of the story. Although the film is now believed lost, the evocative catalog description provides valuable insight into the narrative:

> Scene, a country garden. Enter an old man carrying a canvas chair, which he places to his satisfaction in a quiet corner and settles himself with a book for a comfortable afternoon. But the heat proves oppressive, the book drops from his fingers,

and he falls asleep. A mischievous boy next enters, carrying in his hand a very formidable Chinese cracker; this he places surreptitiously under the chair, and, after quietly lighting the fuse, he runs away. There is a few moments' pause and then a terrific explosion, and as the smoke clears away it is found that the chair and the occupant have entirely disappeared. A few moments more and they begin to come down in bits, first an arm and leg, and then the bits of the chair and the remainder of the body fall through the air on the scene of the explosion.

By attributing the explosion to the workings of a "Chinese cracker," the sequence implicitly racializes the source of destruction, holding the non-White other culpable for the obliteration of the White body. If, as I am suggesting, the on-screen explosion also functions as a metaphor for the combustibility of celluloid, recognition of which helped prompt Hepworth's shift from a photographic to a plastic conception of the image, then *The Gunpowder Plot*'s equation of the explosion with non-Whiteness can also be read as an inadvertent and displaced acknowledgment of film history's material dependence on the hidden labor of non-White bodies. These include the Black sharecroppers and tenant farmers sustaining the cotton economy that, in turn, fed the manufacture of celluloid—a link only sustained by Zakiyyah Iman Jackson's above-mentioned insights into the tight cultural fit between Blackness and plasticity. From this perspective, *The Gunpowder Plot* can be read as encrypted testimony to the invisible labor of non-White bodies in driving historical transformations in cinematic form.

III.

The claim that celluloid played a critical role in the emergence of motion picture production and projection technologies is far from controversial. As one of the basic components of early photographic film stock, celluloid has been treated extensively both across technical histories and newer, "eco-materialist" histories. In this chapter, however, I have sought to extend these accounts by exploring this pioneering thermoplastic's role not only in sustaining film technology, but in shaping film aesthetics. In doing so, I first emphasized the unpredictable social, economic, discursive, and material agency of an ingredient that, at once a fractious physical body and a function of modern manufacturing processes, came to emblematize both the promise and the peril of modern industrial production, as well as White and Black modernities alike.[66] Then, through an analysis of his early film-oriented writings and early film output, I sought to implicate this ingredient in the evolving aesthetic practice of early pioneering British filmmaker, Cecil M. Hepworth. In particular, I highlighted the role of celluloid in helping the director push past the photographic conception of the cinematic image that initially defined his practice to the more plastic conception of its possibilities embodied in his embrace of trick effects. As this synopsis suggests, this chapter's historical purview is relatively modest, limited to a single period within the career of a single director. Yet I hope that, despite its limitations, the analysis has yielded a model of the relationship between shifting tendencies in early film form and one of the primary ingredients in film technology that can be applied more broadly across the early period—allowing us to explore similar lines of inquiry in relation to silver, and gelatin, and to establish similar connections in the practices of other directors.

Notes

1. Cecil M. Hepworth, "The Idler's Notes," *The Amateur Photographer* 661, vol. XXV (1897): 454.
2. Hepworth, "The Idler's Notes," 454.
3. Hepworth, "The Idler's Notes," 454.
4. Ian Christie, "Time Regained: The Complex Magic of Reverse Motion," in *Projected Shadows: Psychoanalytic Reflections on the Representation of Loss in European Cinema*, ed. Andrea Sabbadini (London: Routledge, 2007), 165.
5. Hepworth, "The Idler's Notes," 454.
6. C. Francis Jenkins, *Animated Pictures: An Exposition of the Historical Development of the Cinematograph* (Washington, DC: H L McQueen, 1898), 5; William Kennedy-Laurie Dickson and Antonia Dickson, *History of the Kinetograph, Kinetoscope, and Kinetophonograph* (New York: Albert Bunn, 1895), 33.

7. For technical histories that track celluloid's application in the development of a flexible, transparent base for filmic emulsions, see Michael Chanan, *The Dream That Kicks: The Prehistory and Early Years of Cinema in Britain* (London: Routledge, 2012), 68–77; Leo Enticknap, *Moving Image Technology: From Zoetrope to Digital* (New York: Wallflower Press, 2005); Deac Rossell, *Living Pictures: The Origins of the Movies* (Albany, NY: SUNY Press, 1998). For a more recent "eco-materialist" history in which the film industry's use of celluloid is part of early cinema's implication in broader environmental practices like resource extraction and media waste account of film's reliance on silver, see Richard Maxwell and Toby Miller, *Greening the Media* (Oxford: Oxford University Press, 2012).
8. Sianne Ngai, *Our Aesthetic Categories: Zany, Cute, Interesting* (Cambridge, MA: Harvard University Press, 2012), 29.
9. Catherine Malabou, *Plasticity at the Dusk of Writing: Dialectic, Destruction, Deconstruction* (New York: Columbia University Press, 2010), 67. The phrase "the plastic arts" covers all art forms involving the moulding of form, whether literally, as in sculpture and ceramics, or figuratively, as in painting, film, and photography.
10. Jeffrey L. Meikle, *American Plastic: A Cultural History* (New Jersey: Rutgers University Press, 1995).
11. Élie Faure, "The Art of Cineplastics," in *French Film Theory and Criticism: 1907–1939*, ed. Richard Abel (New Jersey: Princeton, 1988), 258–267.
12. Meikle, *American Plastics*, 3.
13. Edward Chauncey Worden, *Nitrocellulose Industry: A Compendium of the History, Chemistry, Manufacture, Commercial Application and Analysis of Nitrates, Acetates and Xanthates of Cellulose as Applied to the Peaceful Arts, with a Chapter on Gun Cotton, Smokeless Powder and Explosive Cellulose Nitrates*, vol. II (New York: D. van Nostrand Company), vii–viii.
14. Uncredited, *Cellulose as a Base for Artificial Teeth* (New York: Celluloid Manufacturing Company, 1878), 3–4.
15. Tom Gunning, "Tracing the Individual Body: Photography, Detectives, and Early Cinema," in *Cinema and the Invention of Modern Life*, eds. Lee Charney and Vanessa R. Schwarz (Berkeley, CA: University of California Press, 1996), 17.
16. Meikle, *American Plastics*, 1.
17. Robert Friedel, *Pioneer Plastic: The Making and Selling of Celluloid* (Madison: University of Wisconsin Press, 1983), 15.
18. Editorial, "Explosive Teeth," *New York Times*, September 16, 1874, 4; Uncredited, "Dangers of Celluloid," *Scientific American* 66, no. 14 (1892): 208; Harmanus Fisher, "Dangers of Celluloid," *Scientific American* 68, no. 3 (1893): 39. Thanks to Deac Rossell for these references. See Deac Rossell, "Exploding Teeth, Unbreakable Sheets and Continuous Casting: Nitrocellulose from Gun-Cotton to Early Cinema," in *This Film Is Dangerous!*, eds.

Roger Smither and Carol Surowiec (Brussels: International Federation of Film Archives [FIAF], 2003).
19. Catherine Malabou, *Plasticity at the Dusk of Writing: Dialectic, Destruction, Deconstruction* (Columbia University Press, 2010), 67.
20. Steven B. Smith, *Modernity and Its Discontents: Making and Unmaking the Bourgeois from Machiavelli to Bellow* (New Haven, CT: Yale University Press, 2016), 17.
21. Fredrich Engels and Karl Marx, "Manifesto of the Communist Party," in Karl Marx, *The Revolutions of 1848* (London: Pelican Marx Library, 1973), 71; Zygmunt Bauman, *Liquid Modernity* (Cambridge: Polity Press, 2012).
22. Anna Arabindan-Kesson, *Black Bodies, White Gold: Art, Cotton, and Commerce in the Atlantic World* (Durham, NC: Duke University Press, 2021), 159; Zakkiyah Iman Jackson, *Becoming Human: Matter and Meaning in an Anti-Black World* (New York: New York University Press, 2020), 81.
23. Hepworth, *Came the Dawn*, 78.
24. Arabindan-Kesson, *Black Bodies, White Gold*, 162.
25. Cecil M. Hepworth, *Came the Dawn: Memories of a Film Pioneer* (London: Phoenix House, 1951), 31. For more on this early period in Hepworth's career, see Simon Brown, *Cecil Hepworth and the Rise of the British Film Industry 1899–1911* (Exeter: Exeter University Press, 2016).
26. Luke McKernan, *Charles Urban: Pioneering the Non-Fiction Film in Britain and America* (Exeter: University of Exeter Press, 2018), 16–17.
27. While the November 1899 Hepworth catalog that originally listed these titles is now lost, many of the films produced in that year are listed and described in a 1903 Hepworth catalog, which includes a number of films made in previous years, and which is available at the British Film Institute.
28. Georges Méliès, "Kinematographic Views: A Discussion by Georges Melies," trans. Stuart Liebman, in André Gaudreault, *Film and Attraction* (Springfield, IL: University of Illinois Press, 2011), 138–139. See, for example, Mary Ann Doane, *The Emergence of Cinematic Time* (Cambridge, MA: Harvard University Press, 2002); Oliver Gaycken, *Devices of Curiosity: Early Cinema and Popular Science* (Oxford: Oxford University Press, 2015); Charles Musser, *The Emergence of Cinema: The American Screen to 1907* (Berkeley: University of California Press, 1994).
29. Tom Gunning, "The Transforming Image," *Pervasive Animation*, ed. Suzanne Buchan (London: Routledge, 2013), 54.
30. Gunning, "The Transforming Image," 55.
31. Tom Gunning, "'Primitive' Cinema: A Frame-up? or The Trick's on Us," in *Cinema Journal* 28, no. 2 (1989): 3.
32. Jonathan Crary, *Techniques of the Observer: On Vision and Modernity in the Nineteenth Century* (Cambridge, MA: MIT Press, 1992), 16; Gunning, "'Primitive' Cinema.'"

33. Gunning, "The Cinema of Attractions," 382. As Mary Ann Doane has put this, to claim that film's earliest screenings functioned primarily as exhibitionistic "demonstrations of the capabilities of the machine itself" is not to make any final ruling on the nature of the capabilities being represented—where "one of the most prominent capabilities exhibited was that of indexicality, the ability to *represent* motion and temporal duration." Doane, *The Emergence of Cinematic Time*, 24–25.
34. Distinctions between these two approaches were very significant to viewers of the day, from Georges Brunel's description on Méliès's "fantastic scenes" as "a special genre, entirely distinct from the ordinary cinematographic views consisting of street scenes or genre subjects," to Cecil M. Hepworth's clear distinction between "cinema extraordinary" and "'the usual thing'" in animated photography. (Georges Brunel, qtd. in Miriam Rosen, "Méliès, Georges," in John Wakeman, *World Film Directors: Volume I, 1890–1945* [New York: The H. W. Wilson Company, 1987], 747–776; Hepworth, "The Idler's Notes," 454.) And these distinctions are still at play today. See, for example, Richard Abel's distinction between work that "record[s]" and works that "displayed the 'magical properties of the cinematic apparatus as … spectacle"; Frank Kessler's suggestion that, while all films involve a trick, in the *scènes a trucs*, the trick effects are "clearly foregrounded"; and Gunning's own recent acknowledgment that, while "one must resist creating a rigid dichotomy between realism and fantasy," formal distinctions between "the freedom of reference possible in drawn or painted animation [and] photography's automatic reference to some prefigured reality" nevertheless hold. (Richard Abel, *The Ciné Goes to Town: French Cinema, 1896–1914, Updated and Expanded Edition* [Berkeley: University of California Press, 1998], 62; Frank Kessler, "Trick Films," in *Encyclopedia of Early Cinema*, ed. Richard Abel [New York: Routledge, 2005], 932; Gunning, "The Transforming Image," 54.)
35. Simon Brown, *Cecil Hepworth and the Rise of the British Film Industry 1899–1911* (Exeter: Exeter University Press, 2016), 25–26.
36. Cecil M. Hepworth, *Animated Photography: The ABC of the Cinematograph*, 2nd Edition (Ludgate Hill: Hazel, Watson and Viney, 1900 [1897]), 1, 4. Italics mine.
37. Crary, *Techniques of the Observer*, 36.
38. Crary, *Techniques of the Observer*, 50.
39. Hepworth, *Animated Photography*, 4.
40. Hepworth, *Animated Photography*, 83.
41. Enticknap, *Moving Image Technology*, 12.
42. Hepworth, *Animated Photography*, 84–85. Italics mine.
43. Tom Gunning, "The Impossible Body of Early Film," in *Corporeality in Early Cinema: Viscera, Skin, and Physical Form*, eds. Marina Dahlquist, Doron

Galili, Jan Olsson, and Valentine Robert (Bloomington: Indiana University Press, 2018), 11.
44. William Brown and David H. Fleming, *The Squid Cinema from Hell: Kinoteuthis Infernalis and the Emergence of Chthulumedia* (Edinburgh: Edinburgh University Press, 2020), 13.
45. Kessler, "Trick Film," 931.
46. Hepworth, *Animated Photography*, 79, 81.
47. For a review of philosophies of fire, from Heraclitus to Bachelard, see Isobel Armstrong, "Fire," *19: Interdisciplinary Studies in the Long Nineteenth Century* 25 (2017). http://doi.org/10.16995/ntn.801
48. Catherine Malabou, *Plasticity at the Dusk of Writing: Dialectic, Destruction, Deconstruction* (New York: Columbia University Press, 2010), 67.
49. Hepworth, "The Idler's Notes," 454. As he would note more than thirty years later, "the French ... had held for so long the field of exciting tricks." (Hepworth, *Came the Dawn*, 121).
50. "Chapeaugraphy" was a novelty act in which circular pieces of felt were manipulated to resemble different kinds of hats. For discussions of just some of these intersections between early cinematic practices and visual culture, conceived broadly, see Scott Curtis, Philippe Gauthier, Tom Gunning, and Joshua Yumibe, eds., *The Image in Early Cinema: Form and Material* (Bloomington: Indiana University Press, 2018).
51. Hepworth, *Came the Dawn*, 17.
52. Hepworth, *Animated Photography*, 79.
53. The other is *The Conjurer and the Boer*. Overall information about Hepworth's 1900 output drawn from John Barnes, *The Beginnings of the Cinema in England, 1894–1901: 1900* (Exeter: Exeter University Press, 1997), Appendix 1: British Films of 1900.
54. The precise month in 1900 is identified in Denis Gifford, *British Film Catalogue: Two Volume Set—The Fiction Film/The Non-Fiction Film* (London: Routledge, 2016).
55. This 1903 Hepworth catalogue is available at the British Film Institute.
56. Hepworth, *Came the Dawn*, 31.
57. Gunning, "'Primitive' Cinema?," 7.
58. Bazin, "Ontology of the Photographic Image," 14.
59. Doane, *The Emergence of Cinematic Time*, 231; André Bazin, "The Evolution of the Language of Cinema," *What is Cinema?*, ed. and trans. Hugh Gray (Berkeley: University of California Press, 2005), 35.
60. Tom Gunning, "Crazy Machines in the Garden of Forking Paths: Mischief Gags and the Origins of American Film Comedy," in *Classical Hollywood Comedy*, eds. Kristine Brunovska Karnick and Henry Jenkins (New York: Routledge, 2013), 90.
61. Connor, *The Matter of Air*, 307.

62. Kristin Whissel, *Spectacular Visual Effects: CGI and Contemporary Cinema* (Durham, NC: Duke University Press, 2014).
63. This may be why pyrotechnic spectacles have served historically as a showcase of cinema's capacity to present spatio-temporal experiences that diverge from the human perceptual norm, through devices like slow-motion. For more on this, see Pansy Duncan, "'Journeys of Adventure among Its Far-Flung Debris': Three Theories of the Blockbuster Explosion Spectacle," *JCMS: Journal of Cinema and Media Studies* 59, no. 2 (2020): 1–22.
64. Tom Gunning, "The Impossible Body of Early Film," in *Corporeality in Early Cinema: Viscera, Skin, and Physical Form*, eds. Marina Dahlquist, Doron Galili, Jan Olsson, and Valentine Robert (Bloomington: Indiana University Press, 2018), 20.
65. Gunning, "Crazy Machines," 89.
66. Latour, *We Have Never Been Modern*, 2.

Chapter Two
Infected Gelatin and the Bacterial Life of Popular Science Cinema

Around the midpoint of his 1951 memoir, *Came the Dawn*, pioneering British filmmaker Cecil M. Hepworth recalls a disquieting encounter with bacteria in one of his early efforts at large-batch film development. "The trouble," he notes,

> took the form of hundreds of thousands of little faint white spots which appeared all over the film when it was drying. This only happened two or three times, but each time it affected the whole roomful of film at once, and when that was cleared it did not recur in any form until the next time, and then again the whole roomful was spoilt.[1]

While initially confounded, he soon identified the source of the spots, tracing them to a bacterial infection in the gelatin emulsion:

> As I saw it, the air was warm and damp, there was moisture everywhere and here was moist gelatin with a small quantity of glycerine in it to keep it pliable. And the symptom never occurred in small doses: either there was no sign of it or the whole shooting match was affected ... Should I have said infected, I wondered? Here were all the optimum conditions for a gelatin culture of micro-organisms—and in the air there are bacteria everywhere. The films were suffering from a disease which attacked them like an epidemic. Any bacterial disinfectant which would not harm the film ought to scotch the disease. So I added a trace of formaldehyde to the final bath of very diluted glycerine and water, and the trouble disappeared, never again to return.[2]

Hepworth's account of the role of bacterially-infected gelatin in producing "thousands of little faint white spots" rests on inference rather than research. Yet the scene of infected gelatin he describes in this passage anticipates later scientific accounts of the phenomenon. The coating of choice for photographic and motion picture film stocks for most of the twentieth century, gelatin served at once as a vehicle for light-sensitive silver salts and as a means of binding them to the celluloid base. At the same time, as an animal product derived from the hides, bones, and connective tissue of cattle, sheep, and pigs, gelatin was a breeding ground for microorganisms. While the gelatin production line subjected this raw material to a harsh multistage treatment process, recent studies of gelatin show a significant bacterial load in both food-grade and industrial-grade gelatins, suggesting a link between the fungal markings on Hepworth's stock and the gelatin content of the filmic emulsion.[3] As early as 1905, technical writer Paul Noncree Hasluck was promoting formaldehyde as a means of "hardening the gelatine [sic] films, so as to ... destroy bacteria," with the implication that bacteria remained a problem that demanded almost constant vigilance.[4]

While Hepworth's own output was focused on actualities and short dramatic films, his career coincided with the rise of scientific modes of visualization in which bacteria often played a prominent role. These range in form from films made expressly as popular entertainment to those with an audience of professional scientists in mind. Produced under the auspices of the Charles Urban Trading Company, British naturalist F. Martin Duncan's early *Typhoid Bacteria* (1903) "shows hundreds of typhoid and other disease germs found in sewage-contaminated water, in all stages of growth, and in restless unceasing movement."[5] French microbiologist Jean Comandon's *Ultramicroscope Time-Lapse of Syphilis Parasite* (1910), meanwhile, shows infected hen's blood observed under a microscope, featuring a spontaneous agglutination of syphilis spirochetes. A scientific film that also used microcinematography, the short was produced by Comandon in conjunction with the Pathé Frères film production establishment while also contributing to his research agenda as a medical scientist.[6] Finally, British nature documentarian F. Percy

Smith's *The Fly Pest* (1910), also produced under the umbrella of the Charles Urban Trading Co., casts the fly as at once a vector of disease and the focus of an "aesthetics of wonder."[7] The first act features a life-cycle of flies as they develop from a white mass of eggs laid in putrid meat, into maggots burrowing into the dirt to enter the pupa state; the pupae themselves; the wingless flies emerging from the filth, then fully formed adult flies. The second act of this little life history, entitled "How Flies Carry Contagion," dramatizes recent discoveries about flies' status as carriers of bacteria, flitting quickly from images of flies gathering on rotten fish and swarming on lumps of sugar to an image of a baby placidly sucking a pacifier from which the flies have just departed.

In one prominent early twentieth-century account of dealings with film stock, then, we find instances of bacterially tainted film stock that align with recent research on gelatin's vulnerability to bacterial infection. At the same time, in early twentieth-century practices of science visualization, we find a recurrent interest in capturing the drama of bacterial infection. What is the relationship, if any, between these two registers, the material and the aesthetic? As a constituent of cinema's technological and industrial register, did gelatin touch its aesthetic register in any consistent way?

This chapter explores the link between the early bacteria film and an aspect of motion picture technology that might be expected to connect with it—namely gelatin's vulnerability to infection. Here, however, I approach this relationship slightly differently to the way I approach it elsewhere in this book. In my discussions of silver and celluloid, I represent this relationship as a positive one, ascribing to these materials a formative role in shaping the emergence of early cinema's aesthetic regimes. Yet, as I broach it here, the relationship between the material and aesthetic orders constitutes less an encounter than a non-encounter, in which the gelatin content of motion picture film stock appears, quite conspicuously, *not* to have made any direct impression on the practice of bacteria film. This chapter, then, is ultimately an account of why it hasn't done so, arguing that gelatin's peculiar "politico-material" status played a prominent role in this outcome (although, again, gelatin's role must be set alongside that of other industrial, economic, environmental, and cultural factors). As I will show, while scholars and researchers freely acknowledged gelatin's status as an animal derivative, the substance's animal connections tended to be relegated to the past, in a gesture that disavowed its ongoing susceptibility to the vicissitudes of animal matter such as rot and infection. In other words, at this point in history, gelatin was understood neither as an animal derivative nor as entirely not-animal, but rather as "animal no more." It is in part as a function of this peculiar politico-material profile, I suggest, that gelatin failed to leave a direct trace on motion picture film's aesthetic register—leaving us with a striking non-coincidence between visualizations of bacteria *via* film stock and visualizations of bacteria *in* film stock. I will illustrate this non-coincidence by setting two sets of images side by side: screenshots of a 1909 film by Jean Comandon showing the syphilis spirochete, and images of spots on film stock by prominent Kodak research scientists.[8]

What, then, was filmic gelatin's politico-material constitution? How was this animal derivative produced by and imagined in modern techno-scientific research and industrial manufacturing practices? At a purely material level, the gelatin in filmic emulsions is a natural polymer derived primarily from collagen found in animal connective tissues such as skin, bones, and cartilage. While food-grade gelatin was—and still is—widely used in foodstuffs, from ice-cream to gravy, film-grade gelatin needed to be refined far "beyond the requirements of edible gelatin and far, far beyond those of its humble relation, glue."[9] Indeed, the gelatin manufacturing process involved a relentless cycle of liming, washing, neutralizing, cooking, clarifying, concentrating, cooling, drying, and packing, a process designed, in part, to rid it of impurity and/or imperfection. As pioneering film historian Antonia Dickson noted in 1902, the material that resulted was characterized by a "delicate plasticity"—that is to say, by qualities of transparency, stability, and non-reactivity that were put to excellent use in its role as an emulsion.[10] However, despite the measures put in place to perfect it, film-grade gelatin was not without its liabilities. One 1918 paper by Eastman Kodak's in-house emulsion scientists documents cases in which "the wet gelatin layer becomes more or less finely wrinkled or corrugated" after exposure to liquid, whether as a result of hot, humid weather or during washing.[11] Similarly, a 1927 paper from the same source itemizes the risks of improperly stored or produced gelatin, including the tendency to strip away from the base, to curl up or frill at the edges, and, in hot weather, to dissolve or melt.[12] And perhaps most significant for our purposes is the fact—little-documented in the scientific literature of the day, but increasingly borne out by gelatin science today—that the material remained susceptible to disease and decay.

Yet if this was the strictly material logic of filmic gelatin, understanding the substance at a broader politico-material level requires understanding the erasure under which some aspects of this logic were put. Nicole Shukin's *Animal Capital* has advanced one influential account of this erasure, arguing that "the animal origins of film stock rarely erupted into historical consciousness"—and there is no denying that, in the popular imagination, gelatin's contingency on animal slaughter and disassembly was rarely acknowledged.[13] Shukin's book provides a clear-eyed analysis of the "strategies of sensory and affective containment" used to effect this repression, noting that "the rendering industry has innovated many material technologies for scrubbing itself clean of the acrid, malodorous signs of its carnal commerce."[14] Over the course of the twentieth century, for example, many gelatin manufacturers traded busy urban environments for isolated rural ones, while factory design prioritized efforts to limit "olfactory leakage from the industrial cooking of animal remains."[15] But while everyday consumers of gelatin were shielded from the scenes of industrialized carnage on which its manufacture was contingent, standard work in emulsion research eagerly enumerated them. References to the "animal origins" of the substance, including such specific parts as "bones," "ears, cheek-pieces, pates," and "hides" appear frequently in the work of Samuel E. Sheppard, an emulsion scientist in the Kodak Research Laboratories, and author of the 1925 technical handbook *Gelatin in Photography*.[16] The opening gambit of its second chapter, "Manufacturing Processes," is the rather bald claim that "gelatin and its humbler relative, glue, are products of animal origin, the result of the action of hot water or steam upon certain tissues and structures of the body."[17] It was very much as an animal by-product that gelatin became a go-to ingredient in the food and pharmaceutical as well as film industries.

What contemporary motion picture scientists elided, I argue, was not the substance's animal origins, or even the obscenities of industrial-scale slaughter that predicate it. Rather, they elided gelatin's *continuing* status as an organic animal ingredient, treating the finished product as a sterile ingredient that had been purged of its biological origins. And to the extent that the clearest sign of the substance's biological origins was its susceptibility to disease and decay, it should come as little surprise that, while gelatin's ongoing vulnerability to infection is common knowledge today, it was rarely recognized in early twentieth-century emulsion research circles. According to an article entitled "Gelatin is Simple Stuff," commissioned by Eastman Kodak for a broad, external audience

> For nearly 45 years it was assumed that gelatin's only job was to serve as a comfortable, practical environment for photography's star performers—the microscopic photo-sensitive silver salts. It had to be good gelatin, of course, refined beyond the requirements of edible gelatin and far, far beyond those of its humble relation, glue. But still, it was generally believed that gelatin's role in the photographic process was wholly passive. It merely sat there, quietly clutching billions of bits of silver halide.[18]

This passage describes two related beliefs about gelatin that dominated cinema's first forty-five years, both of them significant for an understanding of gelatin's politico-material status. The first is the belief that photographic gelatin had achieved a transcendent state of "refine[ment]" that situated it in a realm "beyond" that of edible gelatin and "far, far beyond" that of glue, purifying it of its organic status through a rigorous multistage process of extraction, pretreatment, hydrolysis, and recovery. The second is that, as a result, gelatin had been stripped of its capacity to act, transformed from ingredient to "environment": "gelatin's role in the photographic process was wholly passive. It merely sat there, quietly clutching billions of bits of silver halide." In this view, purged of its animal connections, gelatin was merely the sterile, recumbent vehicle for "photography's star performers—the microscopic photo-sensitive silver salts."

This insistence on film-grade gelatin's sterile, non-organic status shapes Sheppard's 1923 tome, *Gelatin in Photography, Volume I.* Yes, Sheppard acknowledges the presence of bacteria in the raw material, warning that, absent proper precautions, "bacteria will ruin everything."[19] Yet he also insists that bacteria can be vanquished through a relentless cycle of liming, washing, neutralization, cooking, clarifying, concentration, bleaching, cooling, and drying that he sets out in his account of the manufacturing process. Liming, for example, "saponifies fatty material, removes dirt, and dissolves blood and shreds of flesh, besides acting as a mild antiseptic to help preserve the stock."[20] Drying at a temperature below 20° Celsius, meanwhile, enables the maker to avoid "infection."[21] In prescribing these steps, Sheppard emphasizes the high standards of cleanliness and sterility required in order to maintain the purity of the product, from the "sterility of water used," to the "sterility of containers, transporting vessels" and the "relative sterility of air, in drying."[22] The ultimate implication is that the gelatin manufacturing process serves to neutralize its organic component, converting it from animal by-product to inorganic stuff. At one point, for example, Sheppard quotes Humphrey Davy's contention that "'After animal substances are subjected to the action of lime they cease to become putrescible; they resist putrefaction,'" since lime "has a strong preservative and a decidedly antiseptic power, which arrests putrefaction."[23] To the extent that all animal matter has the potential for putrefaction under the right conditions, the claim that lime helps the stock "resist putrefaction" suggests an underlying assumption that gelatin has escaped its animal origins.[24] This assumption, in turn, is supported by the belief that gelatin lacks inherent qualities of its own, that it is not a "chemical substance of definite composition and constitution. . . . But a material embodying a history, which, from first to last, affects its behavior."[25]

This vision of gelatin as "animal no more" crystallizes in a pair of studies, both published a decade or so after the rise of the popular science film, that at once register and rule out the effects of infected gelatin. In the first of these articles, Kodak Eastman research scientists J. I. V. Crabtree and G. E. Matthews set out to identify the "factors influencing moisture markings"—that is, the "objectionable defects" formed on the emulsion side of motion picture film "when droplets of water come into contact with [it] either before or after the film is exposed ... if all superfluous moisture is not removed from the film before drying or if the rate of drying is changed during the progress of drying."[26] As a series of illustrative figures shows, the marks themselves varied in color and kind, ranging from white spots with smooth edges, to white spots with serrated edges and white spots with black rings. The authors do not offer a clear conclusion as to the source of the marks: while suggesting that they might be the effect of a process of desensitization brought about by water exposure, they also note potential problems with this reading. As they observe, it "is difficult to explain" the fact that the "same substance, water, should at the same time cause black and white spots" without reference to some intervening substance.[27] What is striking for our purposes is Crabtree and Matthews' reluctance to concede that bacterial growth on the surface of the gelatin might have played a role in this respect. In the recorded discussion, a Mr. Renwick advances just such a suggestion, noting

> I have had some experiences showing how quickly some bacteria will get to work, and when one remembers how difficult it is to sterilize gelatine, it is not surprising if one occasionally gets desensitizing or reducing products formed during their life processes.[28]

The respondent also remarks that one of the pieces of film stock "had been stored under warm semi-moist conditions. On that one particularly I thought I could recognize definite fungus growth."[29] Yet the authors are oddly insistent on the non-relation between the spots and any trace of bacterial activity. While conceding that they "have not made any definite experiments," they nevertheless conclude that "it is doubtful, especially with the emulsions with which we are dealing."[30]

Gelatin's status as a potential breeding ground for bacteria extended to its status as the occasion for the growth of sulphides in the developer—that is, the group of chemicals responsible for converting a latent image to a visible image. Yet even among scientists who undertook to scrutinize the presence of sulphides in developing solutions, there is a refusal to acknowledge the possibility that gelatin may have played a role. Consider, for example, a 1924 study of "fogging" in developing solution opened and left in bottles, tubes, or tanks or developing machines by Eastman Kodak colleagues J. I. Crabtree and Merle L. Dundon.[31] There, the authors accurately ascribe the fogging effect to the working of bacteria, noting that "A sample of the fogging developer from the tank after standing . . . [was] found to contain numerous organisms . . . A second sample obtained from the tank just as the first trace of fog became evident showed much the same bacterial flora as the first."[32] Yet when it comes to speculating about the source of the bacteria, Crabtree and Dundon propose that "the organisms were probably introduced with the water."[33] While reflecting that "gelatine [sic] dissolved from the film [may act] as food for the organisms," the authors do not pursue this line of inquiry.[34]

These readings of contemporary motion picture engineering science help underscore gelatin's politico-material status as an animal derivative that is coded as animal-no-more. One effect of this status is the fact that the ingredient's purely material effects become illegible to those tasked with deciphering them. But what was the foundation of this conception of gelatin? The answer, I suggest, is that it was predicated on a vision of motion picture technology as machine *as opposed to* organism—a vision that gelatin's ongoing susceptibility to bacterial infection would seem to threaten. The dichotomy between machine and organism, of course, dates back at least as far as Immanuel Kant's *Critique of Judgment*, which provides a number of bases for the distinction. The first is that whereas a machine's parts interact purposelessly, the parts of an organism "work toward the purpose of the organism as a whole."[35] The second is that, whereas a living organism "interacts creatively with its environment, adapting to it in order to survive," machines "interact blindly with their environment."[36] This Kantian framework implicitly celebrates the creativity, purposiveness, and holism of the organism as against the blindness, contingency, and non-purposiveness of the machine.

Yet it was the figure of the machine that, in both scientific and aesthetic circles in the early twentieth century, had a premium in accounts of motion picture film technology. In the context of scientific forms of visualization, researchers championed the mechanical character of still and motion picture photography on the basis that it transcended the limitations of the flesh and the obfuscations of subjectivity. As Lorraine Daston and Peter Galison have shown in their work on "mechanical objectivity," this epistemic ideal, which rose to favor in the eighteenth century, "combatted the subjectivity of scientific and aesthetic judgment, dogmatic system building, and anthropomorphism," and, as such, "it took on a moral aspect" as a charm "against ambiguity, bad faith, and system building."[37] In the context of art and entertainment cinema, meanwhile, critics championed the mechanical character of motion picture photography as a source of revelatory power. For Walter Benjamin, cinema served to "expand" space and "extend" movement, while "bring[ing] to light entirely new structures of matter."[38] For André Bazin, film's mechanical capacity to generate images without human intervention afforded it the power to "strip its object of ... piled up preconceptions, that spiritual dust and grime with which my eyes have covered it."[39] And for Dziga Vertov, the camera was best understood as a "kino-eye, more perfect than the human eye," capable of feats of perception unavailable to unaided human vision. In other words, both scientific and aesthetic approaches to the filmic image had a powerful investment in a model of the cinema as a machine rather than a living organism. This was arguably compounded by a concern to protect the racial character of cinema as a space of Whiteness. As Kirsty Dootson has argued, in the early twentieth century, animality tended to be equated with non-White bodies; from this perspective, to recognize the presence of animal products in film stock was to compromise cinema's imaginative "align[ment] with the White body."[40]

In what follows, I will show how this non-organic, post-biological vision of gelatin becomes visible at cinema's aesthetic register precisely to the extent that gelatin has failed to make a material impact on visualizations of bacteria in film stock. This failure, I suggest, is an index of the force of the disavowal of the substance's ongoing animal status. By way of arguing this, I will compare two sets of visualizations of what, by all accounts, are bacteria: a popular science short entitled *Spirochaeta Pallida* (1909) by French microbiologist and filmmaker Jean Comandon depicting the movement of syphilis spirochetes, the bacteria that causes syphilis; and the photographic images of markings on film stock that accompany the aforementioned article by Kodak research scientists Crabtree and Matthews.

Produced by Comandon in conjunction with Pathé Freres, *Spirochaeta Pallida* emerged from Comandon's medical research into the possibility of "a reliable diagnostic method for identifying the syphilis spirochete."[41] While the syphilis-causing spirochete had been identified several years earlier, diagnosing the disease remained a challenge, not only, as Oliver Gaycken explains, "because the disease, nicknamed 'the Great Imitator,' mimics other diseases but also because it typically has a long latency period."[42] However, while studying over 500 samples of blood, semen, phlegm, and other bodily fluids using the ultramicroscope (an innovative tool that enabled the visualization of particles smaller than the wavelength of light), Comandon observed that the syphilis spirochete exhibited a distinctive, undulating motion, and turned to film as an ideal medium for recording these findings.[43] Comandon's efforts to capture microscopic life on film quickly acquired the support of Pathé, of the company Pathé Frères, who invited Comandon to work in his production laboratories at Vincennes on the condition that he contribute to Pathé's film catalog.

Spirochaeta Pallida, then, was shot with an innovative camera system that the studio patented in tandem with Comandon, the so-called ultra-microcinematographic camera. The central innovation of this camera was that it conjoined the camera and ultramicroscope, with gears making it possible to move the camera to follow motion within the microscopic frame. The film also had a unique lighting setup. As one French critic explained at the time, whereas the ordinary microscope uses "Perpendicular lighting . . .

where the underside of the preparation is revealed by transparency and stands out in their mass against the claret of the background," the ultra-microcinematographic camera uses "lateral illumination … where the details of the preparation are revealed by refraction and reflection of light rays striking their contours."[44] The upshot of this, as Comandon himself explained in an article in the scientific journal *Comptes rendus hebdomadaires des séances*, was that "the field is black and the objects appear with very bright outlines," providing a uniquely cinematic aesthetic in which the bacteria glimmers a ghostly white against a dark background.[45] In a frame-grab from the film, shown in Figure 2.1, the spiral-shaped spirochete bacteria register as a series of fine, crinkled lines half a millimetre thick, weaving energetically between larger cellular bodies that show up as clusters of glowing white rings. The drama of the film in which they star is not complex: the spirochetes wiggle and squirm across what an intertitle instructs us is the cornea of an eye; the more intrepid

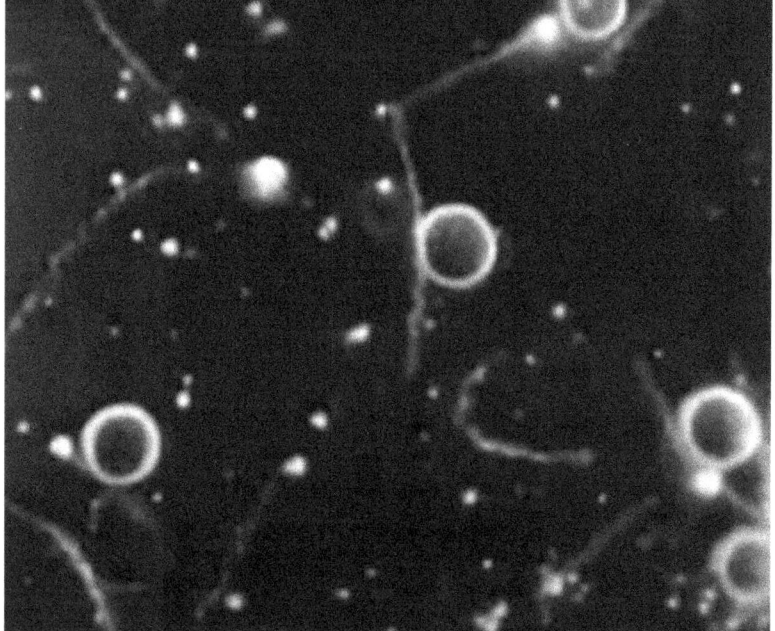

Figure 2.1 Jean Comandon's *Spirochaeta Pallida* (1909) depicts syphilis spirochetes as a series of fine, crinkled lines moving among large, luminous cellular bodies.

among them twitch out of the frame, eager to explore; two spirochetes embrace; and the film cuts to black. Yet when presented to an audience at the French Academy of Science in 1909, the film was a sensation. Reviews in the popular press invoked an aesthetic of wonder to capture the sense that, thanks in part to the technological innovations of the ultra-microcinematographic camera, the film had made the invisible visible.[46]

Against Comandon's film, I set a series of illustrative images from Crabtree and Matthews' "A Study of the Markings on Motion Picture Film," depicting frames of motion picture film stock affected by mysterious markings that I contend were likely the result of bacterially infected gelatin (see Figure 2.2 and Figure 2.3). The markings vary in kind: some form long, tube-like structures surrounded by a kind of aureole, reminiscent of the effects of Man

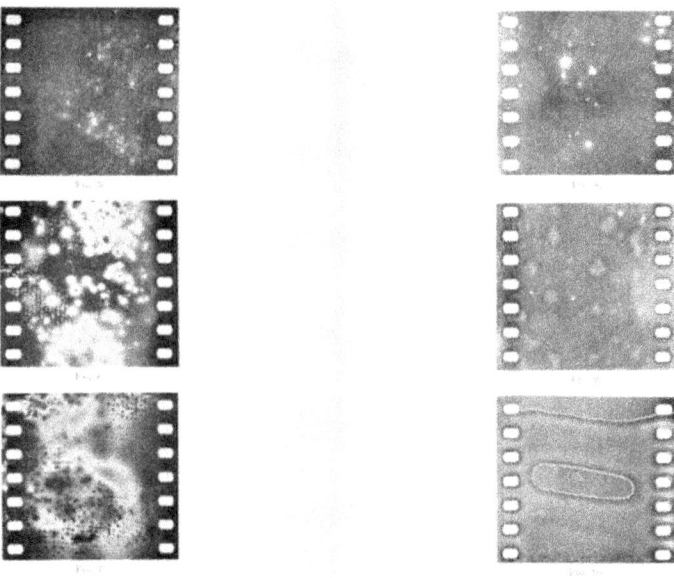

Figure 2.2 Included in an article published in *Transactions of the Society of Motion Picture Engineers* by two Eastman Kodak research scientists, these images show frames of motion picture film stock affected by mysterious markings that I contend were likely the result of bacterially infected gelatin. Source: Media History Digital Library.

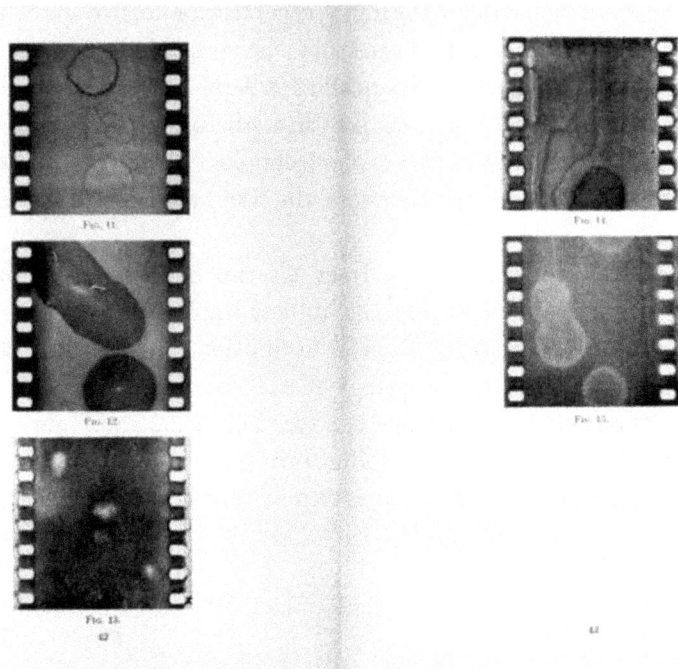

Figure 2.3 Included in an article published in *Transactions of the Society of Motion Picture Engineers* by two Eastman Kodak research scientists, these images show frames of motion picture film stock affected by mysterious markings that I contend were likely the result of bacterially infected gelatin. Source: Media History Digital Library.

Ray's "solarizations"; others form peanuts or globular shapes; yet others are smudgy and formless. There is also a diversity of spots. Some are pin-prick small, others substantial; some gather in clusters, while others are evenly spread; some are black with white halos, while others form throbbing white stars. In some images, the edges of the spots are serrated and spiky, while in others, they are smooth; still others are mottled, "of slightly lighter density inside with slightly heavier density outside than the surrounding film," as Crabtree and Matthews describe it.[47] In all cases, the markings extend across the full width of the film strip, winding their way around the sprocket holes that puncture the edges of the film.

There are striking resonances between the short film *Spirochaeta Pallida* and the set of photographic images of markings on film stock supplied by Crabtree and Matthews. Both texts show bacteria nestling in a dermal or quasi-dermal surface, whether the skin of the human body, or the "skin" of the emulsion (itself a product of animal hides). The analogy between film and skin has been an object of concern for a range of thinkers, including film theorist Laura U. Marks and philosopher Jean-Lucy Nancy. For Marks, for example, the concept of the "skin of the film" captures both the screen's status as "impressionable and conductive, like skin" and its capacity to generate a haptic form of reception that awakens tactile memory.[48] For Nancy, meanwhile, the observation that the French term for a strip of film stock is *pellicule*, literally, "small skin," provides a leaping-off point for an account of film as a diaphanous, skin-like membrane that is "thinness and nothing else."[49] While neither thinker connects film's skin-like qualities to gelatin as one of the primary ingredients of filmic emulsions, or comments on another key feature that the "skin of the film" shares with skin proper (namely, the potential for decay), their efforts to draw a connection between stock and skin speak to the convergences between the Comandon film and the Crabtree and Matthews stills. Indeed, these synchronicities between skin and stock are heightened by the fact that the glancing, lateral light cast on the ultramicroscopic work in Comandon's *Spirochaeta Pallida* leaves us with the image of microscopic life glowing against a black backdrop—much like the images of film stock marked and stained by bacteria. As a result of this "dark-field" illumination technique, *Spirochaeta Pallida* could plausibly pass as an anti-illusionist structural/materialist film, showing the activity of bacteria on the surface of the strip of motion picture film, rather than an event depicted via the strip through the exposure of light-sensitive chemicals to the light.

However, more significant for our purposes than the similarities between these two visualizations of bacteria are the differences between them. Consider that these visualizations might, under other historical circumstances, have intersected and overlapped more than they do. Like all bacteria, bacteria in infected gelatin-bromide film stock are mobile, capable of twitching, wriggling, and gliding on solid surfaces.[50] For Crabtree and Matthews, then, time lapse microcinematography might have yielded a film with significant visual affinities with Comandon's *Spirochaeta Pallida*. And yet these visualizations are radically divergent. What form do these differences take? Perhaps most profoundly, the spirochetes depicted by the short film are in motion, whereas the bacteria depicted photographically in the gelatin emulsion are static. Importantly for our purposes, underpinning this disparity is not a difference in the mobility of the forms themselves, but a difference in the choice of medium used to depict them. While the movements of their syphilitic brethren were captured by a film camera, the movements of the bacteria in gelatin are documented in a series of still images, and thus "suspended" by the stasis of still photography. A different means of visualizing bacterially-infected gelatin could well have yielded movement in ways that would have drawn attention to potential points of connection between the infection-prone gelatin in film stock and the rise of the bacteria film. However, the divergent media used to capture these two objects preclude these potential links.

Yet this medial difference—this non-encounter between these two objects of scientific visualization—itself speaks to the "mark" left by the politico-material constitution of gelatin as a material that is animal-no-more on film aesthetic. For the choices of these two media were driven by, and reinforced, existing presumptions about syphilis bacteria, on the one hand, and gelatin, on the other. Crabtree and Matthews's use of still photography appears to be animated in part by the belief that the gelatin emulsion that bore these infections was a lifeless component-part of a machine—contingent, non-purposive, blind, and incapable of the kind of spontaneous movement that would benefit from capture by moving-image film. By contrast, according to Hannah Landecker, Comandon was prompted to turn to microcinematography by a growing sense of the "life" of the syphilis bacteria. Where living organisms were known to be subject to spontaneous "modifications... [and] evolution," moving image technology, in this case microcinematography, was appropriate to their depiction.[51] In turn, as Landecker has shown, the use of ultra-microcinematography served to reinforce bacteria's emerging status as a set of microscopic life forms "enhancing the temporal dimension of perception" and functioning, to quote Comandon himself, as a vehicle for biological units "in their living state."⁵² These divergent choices of media, then, only fortify the assumptions that underpinned them—the animating effect of moving image film bolstering syphilis bacteria's claim to life, even as the de-animating effect of the still photograph consigns bacteria-bearing gelatin to what Landecker calls the "'anatomical era' of fixatives and stains."⁵³

The non-convergence between Comandon's *Spirochaeta Pallida* and Crabtree and Matthews's images of gelatin-infected film stock could easily be enlisted as a sign that there is no relation between the early popular science film's preoccupation with bacteria on the one hand, and film stock gelatin's susceptibility to bacteria on the other. This chapter, however, has sought to complicate this all-too-available reading. Yes, as I have shown, appreciation of gelatin's ongoing vulnerability to disease and decay was foreclosed by a widespread commitment to a vision of gelatin as "animal-no-more" (which itself reflected prevailing understandings of film technology as machine rather than organism). This made the effects of gelatin's animal origins almost illegible to early twentieth-century motion picture scientists like Crabtree and Matthews, whose reliance on the still image in depicting filmic emulsions only further embedded assumptions about gelatin's lack of life. Yet, in this respect, the lack of explicit evidence does not undermine this book's argument for the connection between cinema's eco-material underpinnings and its aesthetic logics. On the contrary, the non-relation between film stock gelatin and the bacteria film that I have unpacked here testifies to the powerful impact of a very distinctive, post-organic vision of gelatin on cinema's aesthetic register.

Notes

1. Cecil M. Hepworth, *Came the Dawn: Memories of a Film Pioneer* (London: Phoenix House, 1951), 78.
2. Hepworth, *Came the Dawn*, 79.
3. Elke De Clerck and Paul De Vos, "Study of the Bacterial Load in a Gelatine Production Process Focussed on Bacillus and Related Endosporeforming Genera," *Systematic and Applied Microbiology* 25, no. 4 (2002): 611–617.

4. Paul Nooncree Hasluck, *The Book of Photography: Practical, Theoretic and Applied* (London: Cassell and Company, Ltd, 1905), 457.
5. *Charles Urban Trading Co. Ltd. Catalogue, 1903* (London: Charles Urban, 1903), 86.
6. Hannah Landecker, "Cellular Features: Microcinematography and Film Theory," *Critical Inquiry* 31, no. 4 (2005): 908.
7. Oliver Gaycken, *Devices of Curiosity: Early Cinema and Popular Science* (Oxford: Oxford University Press, 2015), 11.
8. The contemporary American filmmaker Bill Morrison is an avant-garde filmmaker whose work arguably seeks to underscore the medium's organic status. Exemplary here is his 2002 film *Decasia: The State of Decay*, which re-edits decaying silent film footage into a new narrative about mortality, both human and cinematic.
9. KHC, box 39, folder 11, "Gelatin Is Simple Stuff," 13–14.
10. Antonia Dickson, quoted in Paul Spehr, *The Man Who Made Movies* (Washington: John Libbey Publishing, 2008), 125.
11. S. E. Shepperd and F. A. Elliott, "The Reticulation of Gelatin," *Motion Picture News*, November 16, 1918, 2975.
12. S. E. Sheppard, "Behavior of Gelatin the Processing of Motion Picture Film," *Transactions of the Society of Motion Picture Engineers (SMPE)* 6, no. 32 (1927): 721.
13. Nicole Shukin, *Animal Capital: Rendering Life in Biopolitical Times* (Minneapolis: University of Minnesota Press, 2009), 111.
14. Shukin, *Animal Capital*, 64, 63.
15. Shukin, *Animal Capital*, 63.
16. S. E. Sheppard, *Gelatin in Photography, Vol. 1* (New York: D. Van Nostrand Company, 1923), 25.
17. Sheppard, *Gelatin in Photography*, 25
18. KHC, box 39, folder 11, "Gelatin is simple stuff," 13–14.
19. Sheppard, *Gelatin in Photography*, 28.
20. Sheppard, *Gelatin in Photography*, 26.
21. Sheppard, *Gelatin in Photography*, 33.
22. Sheppard, *Gelatin in Photography*, 88.
23. Sheppard, *Gelatin in Photography*, 87.
24. Sheppard, *Gelatin in Photography*, 87.
25. Sheppard, *Gelatin in Photography*, 32.
26. J. I. Crabtree and G. E. Matthews, "A Study of the Markings on Motion Picture Film Produced by Drops of Water, Condensed Water Vapor, and Abnormal Drying Conditions," *Transactions of the Society of Motion Picture Engineers*, October, 1923, 29.
27. Crabtree and Matthews, "A Study of the Markings," 37.
28. Crabtree and Matthews, "A Study of the Markings," 45.
29. Crabtree and Matthews, "A Study of the Markings," 45.

30. Crabtree and Matthews, "A Study of the Markings," 45.
31. Merle L. Dundon an J. I. Crabtree, "Investigations on Photographic Developers: Sulphide Fog by Bacteria in Motion Picture Developers," *Transactions of the Society for Motion Picture Engineers*, November, 1924, 28.
32. Dundon and Crabtree, "Investigations on Photographic Developers," 33.
33. Dundon and Crabtree, "Investigations on Photographic Developers," 33.
34. Dundon and Crabtree, "Investigations on Photographic Developers," 33.
35. Malcolm Turvey, "Vertov: Between the Organism and the Machine," *October* 121 (2007): 8.
36. Turvey, "Vertov," 8.
37. Lorraine Daston and Peter Galison, "The Image of Objectivity," *Representations* 40 (1992): 82.
38. Walter Benjamin, *The Work of Art in the Age of Its Technological Reproducibility, and Other Writings on Media* (Cambridge, MA: Harvard University Press, 2008), 37.
39. Andre Bazin and Hugh Gray, "Ontology of the Photographic Image," *Film Quarterly* 13, no. 4 (Summer, 1960), 8.
40. Kirsty Dootson, "Celluloid Skin," in *Film Stock*, ed. Alice Lovejoy, Kirsty Dootson, and Pansy Duncan (Minneapolis, MN: Minnesota University Press, forthcoming).
41. Gaycken, *Devices of Curiosity*, 91–2.
42. Gaycken, *Devices of Curiosity*, 92.
43. Gaycken, *Devices of Curiosity*, 92.
44. Felix Poli, "Microscope et Cinematographie," in *Cine-Journal* 63, November 1, 1909, 5–8.
45. Jean Comandon, "Biological Physics: Cinematography, with the Ultramicroscope of Microbes, Living Things and Moving Particles," in *Comptes Rendes Hebdomadaires des seances*, 1909, 939. As the *British Medical Journal* explained it at the time, "The source of light was an arc of 30 amperes with an automatic regulator; the microscope was provided with a parabolic condenser to give the lateral illumination." ("Special correspondence," *The British Medical Journal*, November 20, 1909, 1498.)
46. *Le Matin*, October 27, 1909.
47. Crabtree and Matthews, "A Study of the Markings," 35.
48. Laura U. Marks, *The Skin of the Film: Intercultural Cinema, Embodiment, and the Senses* (Durham, NC: Duke University Press, 2000), xii.
49. Jean-Luc Nancy, *The Evidence of Film: Abbas Kiarostami* (Brussels: Yves Gevaert Publisher, 2001), 46.
50. Ben L. Feringa, "In Control of Motion: From Molecular Switches to Molecular Motion," *Accounts of Chemical Research* 34, no 6 (2001): 504–513.
51. Jean Comandon, "Le Cinematographie et les Sciences de la Nature," in *Le Cinema, des origines a nos jours*, ed. Henri Fescourt, 313–322 (Paris: Editions du Cygne, 1932), 319.

52. Hannah Landecker, "Microcinematography and the History of Science and Film," *Isis* 97, no. 1 (2006): 125.
53. Hannah Landecker, "Creeping, Drinking, Dying: The Cinematic Portal and the Microscopic World of the Twentieth-Century Cell," *Science in Context* 24, no. 3 (2011): 399.

Chapter Three

Silver Salts and the Aesthetics of Early Studio-Era Hollywood Cinema

I.

In 1948, outspoken émigré director Erich von Stroheim offered a now-famous account of the troubled post-production history of his notorious 1924 exercise in naturalism, *Greed*. According to von Stroheim, a cadre of MGM studio executives, led by Irving Thalberg, had pressured him to cut his gritty, sprawling masterpiece—an attempt to "reproduce life as it actually was"—from its eight-hour, forty-two-reel initial assembly down to a more studio-friendly twelve reels.[1] When he refused, the film was

> given to a cutter at thirty dollars a week who [sic] had never read the book nor the script, and on whose mind was nothing but a hat ... my picture was arbitrarily cut to nine or ten [reels]. The rest of the negative was burned to get the forty-three cents of silver out.[2]

In standard production histories of the film, this anecdote has served to reinforce a familiar narrative about the consolidation of classical Hollywood film aesthetics across the course of the 1920s.[3] For proponents of this narrative, these aesthetic changes were a function of industrial developments in Hollywood's "mode of production," which, between 1914 and 1930, saw the will of the director increasingly subordinated to the will of the producer within a newly integrated studio system.[4] Yet closer attention to von Stroheim's anecdote demands a revision of this narrative. For by the end of the story, it would appear that the director's true object is neither the studio system at large, nor its functionary, the "cutter," but the silver content of the photographic film stock itself—cast here as pettily desirable scrap metal, or, as von Stroheim puts it, "forty-three cents [worth] of silver." In this respect, the reminiscence obliquely suggests a relationship between two things we commonly keep apart. The first is an aesthetic outcome that has become a byword for the vicissitudes of the early studio system. The second is one of the key ingredients of early motion picture film stock—namely, light-sensitive silver halide crystals.

What would it mean to probe this membrane between the motion picture industry's mineral substrate and the aesthetic logic of Hollywood's early studio years? As a constituent of cinema's technological and industrial register, did silver also touch its aesthetic register? Von Stroheim's acrimonious anecdote points to one of the effects this precious metal might have had on post-World War I Hollywood film aesthetics. His narrative directly ties the silver content of film stock to changes in the shape of his text and indeed implicitly to the rise of the standardized mass cultural cinematic commodity. Yet as Sianne Ngai has usefully reminded us, the aesthetic is not just the realm of "objective" textual properties, like style, genre, and narrative. It is also the realm of our "subjective, feeling-based judgments" about them.[5] By Ngai's lights, then, the claim that silver affected film aesthetics implies not only that it shaped cinema at an objective level, but that it affected how we look at, respond to, or evaluate cinema at a subjective and/or social level. And there is evidence that this *was* the case. The lustrous, conductive metal made its way into film titles of the day, with releases like *Silver Treasure* (Rowland V. Lee, 1927), *The Silver King* (T. Hayes Hunter, 1929), *The Silver Shield* (Thompson Meghan, 1927), and *Silver Comes Through* (Lloyd Ingraham, 1927). At the same time, silver pops up in the rubric of the "silver screen," which, ubiquitous across the trade press during the 1920s, suggests that the metal was routinely enlisted as a metonym for the "magic" of film culture itself.[6]

In a bid to "smear" the immaculate face of film aesthetics, then, this chapter will tease out the implications of silver's seeming percolation from the plane of filmic matter to the plane of film aesthetics. To do so, it will return to the early years of the studio system, an era of aesthetic instability in which efforts to consolidate classical Hollywood practices co-existed with the appearance of industrial and aesthetic alternatives.[7] Focusing in particular on the decade or so immediately following World War I (1918–1930), it will argue that silver did not just support the production of movies in Hollywood, but also shaped their aesthetic register—and that it did so in ways that by turns coordinated with and confounded the agency of human technologies, cultures, and industrial formations. To sustain this argument, I will briefly revisit a range of existing scholarship on the classical Hollywood cinema in an effort to ground the claim that the "classical Hollywood style" was essentially a commodity aesthetic that combined a fetishistic or "magical" allure with standardized narrative and formal economies.[8] Then, I will draw on original research across a wide variety of archival sources to intervene in debates about why this contradictory commodity aesthetic gained the stylistic dominance it did. More specifically, I will contend that, thanks to its dual politico-material profile as both a "sentimental commodity" and a "money commodity," silver also played a role in shaping the classical Hollywood cinema's contradictory aesthetic character. This is not to privilege the role of silver over and against the significant and well-documented effects of other forces, including the antinomies of modernity, the development of the so-called "factory" system of production, and the standardization of recording technologies.[9] As a "sentimental commodity" that embodied what Marx describes as the commodity's "magic" force, silver helped support the discourses of film "magic" by which the classical Hollywood cinema of the 1920s laid claim to a mystical transcendence of market logic.[10] And as what Marx calls a "money commodity," silver played a part in fostering these same cinematic practices' all too visible *adherence to* the logic of the market, helping shape the rise of Classical Hollywood narrative economies.[11] As this account suggests, while some of silver's effects on the aesthetics of early Hollywood cinema are objective, in that they bear on the shape and form of the film, others are subjective, in that they bear on viewers' experiences, perceptions, and evaluations of specific films or of Hollywood film culture at large.

In advancing this argument, my aim is twofold. First, I hope to complicate existing understandings of early studio-era film aesthetics. Where established accounts ascribe changes in cinematic form and experience exclusively to industrial, cultural, and/or economic forces, this chapter will underscore the role of this raw geological material. Second, I hope to extend eco-materialist accounts of film history. Where this body of work has focused extensively on the role of natural resources in film infrastructure, technology, production, and distribution, this chapter will reveal their unexpected significance for genealogies of film *aesthetics*. Methodologically, of course, achieving these aims means ascribing to this precious metal a greater quantum of "agency" than is generally attributed to it across existing work in early film history and eco-materialist film studies. Despite their evident differences, these bodies of work share a tendency to treat silver as a passive, quiescent, or instrumentalized supplement to the motion picture industry's representational agendas. This chapter, by contrast, will emphasize what I have called silver's distinctive "politico-material" agency, where agency refers to any entity that can "make a difference, produce effects, alter the course of events."[12] Casting silver as a uniquely modern fusion of "natural" and "human" history, I will emphasize its capacity to act in ways that bypass or confound human design—while also revealing this agency as a function of socially binding practices of production, circulation, and consumption.[13] Throughout, that is, silver will emerge as what Bruno Latour might call a "Gordian knot"—an "imbroglio of science, politics, economy, law, religion, technology, fiction" that is, as Latour puts it, "simultaneously real, like nature, narrated, like discourse, and collective, like society."[14]

II.

By the 1920s, the classical Hollywood narrative cinema was perhaps *the* premier entertainment commodity, a coordinated complex of studio branding, commercial tie-ins and an incipient star system supported by an ever-more "finely-honed publicity machine."[15] It should come as no surprise, then, that the industry's dominant aesthetic practices exemplified the commodity's contradictory tendencies. At the textual level, films exemplifying the "group style" of the early studio era visibly served a market agenda, working both to enable efficiencies of production (through practices of standardization) and to maximize box-office appeal (through practices designed to secure narrative legibility and spectatorial absorption).[16] At the level of reception, by contrast, these films sustained powerful fantasies of *transcending* market edicts—fantasies of "movie magic" often articulated through the rubric of the "silver screen."[17] According to Matthew Solomon, discourses of "movie magic" had gained traction in the very early years of the studio system, as "the magical visual possibilities conjured up by the [early] cinema" of attractions were "channelled into the 'magic' of [narratively integrated] storytelling."[18] Emphasizing film's spontaneous capacity to absorb and enchant, these discourses—promulgated by a bevy of powerful trade and fan organs like *Photoplay*, *Picture-Play*, *Silver Screen*, and *Motion Picture Magazine*—ascribed to cinema what Horkheimer and Adorno have called "the magic of the incomprehensible."[19] In sum, classical Hollywood film aesthetics in the early studio era formed what Robert Ray has called a "site of negotiation" between commerce and captivation, between "the temptations of rationalization on the one hand, [and] the requirements of seduction on the other."[20]

But how did silver, a precious metal embedded in but not reducible to film history's shifting industrial, cultural, and/or economic regimes, help shape classical Hollywood cinema's peculiarly dual aesthetic character? In answering this question, we must first understand that, well before its application to film sensitization processes, silver had a powerful politico-material profile that gave it an agency all its own.[21] And if the aesthetic profile of the film industry was contradictory, so was the politico-material constitution of silver, oscillating as it did between "magic" and "money."

To begin with the first term in this binary: it is worth noting that, across this decade, there were few commodities that more fully embodied what Marx calls the "magic ... that surrounds the products of labour" than silver.[22] For Marx, all commodities possess a certain "magic or necromancy" that derives from the fact that their value on the market (their "exchange value") is (mis)perceived not as a function of social relations of production, consumption and circulation but as a function of their essential characteristics. Yet the "magic" ascribed to silver was of a special kind. Indeed, during this period, silver seemed to have achieved the doubly fetishized status of what Festa has dubbed the "sentimental commodity"—a status that accrues to a subset of commodities that have the capacity to obscure not just the social relations that confer their exchange value, as in standard commodity fetishism, but their implication in systems of exchange in the first place.[23] Silver, in other words, routinely registered as a singular, unique, and auratic metal, untouched by either the sweat of human labor or by the bustle of exchange. This status had a deep history. Like gold, silver was caught up in American national fantasies of liberty and plenty, fantasies tied to the country's long tradition of silver mining and processing and dating back at least to the work of eighteenth-century silversmith and revolutionary Paul Revere.[24] These fantasies, in turn, were racialized, which is to say, they were inextricable from silver's putative status as a "white metal," the unblemished, luminous appearance of which spoke to the logic of moral purity central to colonial ideologies of White racial superiority.[25] While, in reality, the mining sustaining the American film industry was an "ethnically diverse occupation," silver's surface whiteness—and symbolic "Whiteness"—served to elide the brutal and racialized conditions of its extraction and refinement.[26] Yet the perception of silver as magical or transcendent also had a more recent genesis. A spike in disposable income in the prosperous years immediately after World War I had rendered silver increasingly accessible to middle- and working-class Americans.[27]

For these groups, it came to play a pivotal role in social practices such as gift-giving, inheritance, and festivity—practices that involved an "infusion of human particularity into the interchangeability of the commodity."[28] The visions of silver's miraculous singularity sustained by these practices were cemented by personalization methods such as monograms or armorials.[29]

It is the contention of this section of the chapter that the presence of this "sentimental commodity" in film stock helped to sustain a vision of cinema as a space of magical transcendence. In fact, it was arguably silver halides' allure as the imagined source and origin of "movie magic" that is crystallized in the paeans to the "silver screen" that became ubiquitous in the trade and fan press across the 1920s. From 1922 ad copy extolling "the play of light and shadows on the silver screen" to rhapsodic references to "the magic of the silver-sheet" and "silver sheet magic": this marketing rhetoric figures cinema's magical aura as a kind of numinous silvery halo, reminding us that, pre-color, cinema was far from merely "black and white."[30] Admittedly, expressions like the "silver screen" or the "silver sheet" are conventionally traced not to the silver content of film stock, but to the "silver lenticular" projection screens used across the period. Widely used in the early years of the industry, these screens were so named for their use of reflective silver or aluminium fibres to help enhance the brightness and contrast of the image. They are certainly the most obvious source of the popular expression "the silver screen." Yet there is some evidence that this turn of phrase just as often referred to the silver salts in the gelatin emulsion as to the silver thread in the lenticular projection screen. In John L. Cass's account of what he calls "painting the silver sheet," for example, the "painting" in question refers not to painting a screen but to coloring the *film* through toning processes.[31] And photographic and filmmaking handbooks of the day support the implication that the silver "sheet" in question was the film itself rather than the screen against which it would be projected. The extended accounts of color toning in John Scotland's *The Talkies* and Herbert C. McKay's *The Handbook of Motion Picture Photography*, for example, repeatedly refer to the untoned or undyed positive image as the "silver image."[32]

In this sense, as the object of a "double" fetishism that releases it not just from the taint of labor, but from the very system of exchange, film stock's silver content may have helped confer the aura of "magic" embodied in conventional anthems to the "silver screen."

There is no doubt that, in perpetuating fantasies of movie "magic," popular trade and fan journalism of the 1920s was quick to exploit the presence of this "magical" ingredient in photographic emulsions. Key to this process were accounts of the film production workflow that ascribed outsized agency to the soft, conductive metal while downplaying the role of human labor. A 1929 article in *International Photographer* celebrating the arrival in India of "this new and latest magic, this jugglery of celluloid and light," traces what it dubs "India's New Magic" to "the wonders of light-sensitive silver."[33] A 1930 article in the *Pathé Sun* discussing the rise of "pictures in color" announces that "the *magic* of the colour is effected largely by the character of the film," before clarifying that the "character" can be located, in part, in "light-sensitive silver salts."[34] A 1927 article in *Amateur Movie Makers* entitled "Some Secrets of Film Magic," meanwhile, identifies "action" as the essence of drama before going on to claim that the aim of the producer must be to "capture this elusive quality [i.e., 'action'] and lock it safely in *the dancing silver grains* of cine film."[35] In the process, the article doesn't simply afford the "dancing silver grains" the capacity *of* animation, casting them as a vehicle for drama's magical or "elusive quality." It also affords them the capacity *to* animate, ascribing to them a form of choreographed action that is singled out as a source of film magic.

This fetishistic model of film production reaches a zenith in a nearly exactly contemporary article in *Motion Picture Projectionist*. Penned by prominent Kodak representative Franklin Ellis, the article casts silver as "the one material without which there would be no motion picture industry and the absence of which would make it useless to employ thousands of persons and an enormously impressive array of machines in the manufacture of film."[36] In exquisitely hyperbolic fashion, Ellis imputes the entire "motion picture industry"—comprised of both "an enormously impressive array of machines" and "thousands of persons"—to the agency of a precious metal that is present in film stock in microscopic quantities. Overwriting the labour of editors, actors, and crew, the article recalls Jane Bennett's suggestion that the animistic logic of commodity fetishism amounts to "a kind of perceptual disorder," a malady of vision predicated on the skewed proportionality of capitalism itself.[37] Here, then, as elsewhere across the period, publicists and copywriters appropriated silver's own doubly fetishized status to feed fetishized fantasies of cinematic "magic."

These visions of silver as the "magical" source of an equally "magical" moving-image culture were also propagated in the very fora that might be expected to challenge them—namely in the behind-the-scenes photo-gallery tours of raw stock manufacturing plants that were popular in the trade and fan press during this decade. Exemplary here is a 1922 article in the *Exhibitors Herald* about the "romance of filmmaking from the cotton grower to the motion picture studio."[38] Making a mockery of Marx's suggestion that demystification rests on eschewing the "noisy sphere" of consumption in favor of "the hidden abode of production," the article works to mystify the production process itself.[39] And once again silver plays a key role in this process of mystification. Reflecting what Sharon Corwin calls a fantasy of "autogenic production," the article elevates the role of "silver bullion, of which three tons are used weekly at Kodak park" to the status of active producer, the "wellspring of movie magic."[40] At the same time, the use of a passive voice has the effect of expunging workers altogether from the scene, making film stock's raw ingredients the only visible players in the drama of film production: "the cotton is unloaded and passed through huge washers ... the cotton next is fed through chutes ... A great safe containing silver bullion is then shown ... Then the mixing of these crystals ... to form the light sensitive emulsion."[41]

These pseudo-documentary accounts of the film stock manufacturing process weren't limited to the trade press; indeed, they often graced the fan periodicals, and in this context, too, the silver in film stock served to perpetuate notions of film magic. In an advertorial for *Photoplay* entitled "All that Flickers Isn't Gold," for example, the Eastman Kodak Company describes the process of film manufacture

Figure 3.1 *A Movie Trip Through Filmland* (Paul Fenton, 1921) favors shots of raw materials, like the bars of silver depicted here, over images of the workers who help process them.

for the benefit of a popular audience. While the ad copy implicitly promises to demystify the labor of film stock production—"We all realize the tremendous task of producing a movie . . . But few of us understand the process of manufacturing the film itself"—its effect is quite the opposite. It treats silver as the primary or even sole ingredient of film stock: "Maybe you didn't know that the film is made largely of silver—pure silver . . ." And, as in the article discussed above, its reliance on the passive voice serves to evade the question of agency altogether with the effect of downplaying the role of human labor in the film production chain: "Tons of pure silver *are used* each week in the manufacture of photoplay film . . . The picture above shows *the weighing of* the white metal" (italics mine). In the process, silver acquires an enchanted agency that serves to fuel spectatorial fantasies about the magical qualities of the silver screen.[42]

The 1921 Kodak Eastman industrial film, *A Movie Trip Through Filmland* (Paul Fenton), which would have screened as a pre-feature reel, further exemplifies this popular representation of silver as the magical source of an equally magical moving-image culture. While purporting to document the production of motion picture film stock, the film elides human activity in favor of the "agency" of raw materials—from the "4,000,000 pounds of cotton" consumed each year to make the nitrocellulose base, to the three tonnes of silver consumed each week to produce the light-sensitive emulsion (see Figure 3.1). Staging a chiastic exchange between person and thing, this visualization of the production process is deeply fetishistic. But it also situates this film as a limit-case of what Salomé Aguilera Skvirsky has recently and influentially dubbed the "process genre," a genre she describes as conferring "'an air of' magic" on industrial manufacturing processes.[43] For Skvirsky, the process genre's "'. . . air of' magic" derives from its attention to human labor, which the genre either mystifies (by way of extoling the finished product as a function of an artisanal process) or highlights (by way of extoling the Taylorist "labor congealed" in the finished product).[44] Yet in its focus on the materials' apparent capacity to transform into products *in the absence of* human input, *A Trip Through Filmland* flies in the face of Skvirsky's model. At the same time, it shows up the limits of claims about the appeal of early cinema to a public "fascination with the way things worked," as in what Neil Harris calls the "operational aesthetic" and what Paul Young calls a "presentational tradition."[45] According to Harris's account of this tradition, these early cinematic modes catered to the investigative and information-seeking attitudes of Americans at the time, aiming less to sell illusions than to showcase the awe-inspiring technical, material, and industrial accomplishments at play in the illusion's production.[46] Yet, delivering a miraculous rather than an actual vision of the production of photographic film stock, *A Trip Through Filmland* gives the lie to suggestions that early cinematic modes invested in the wonders of technology were truly invested in knowledge about "the way things worked."

Indeed, those accounts of silver's role in film production that affected a more scientific air tended to further overstate silver's miraculous properties. While, as Marx notes, the commodity-form bears "absolutely no connection with the physical nature of the commodity," these quasi-scientific discussions of the film stock manufacturing process sought to collapse the distinction between film stock's exchange-value and its use-value, as if the value of the film itself could be reduced to the biochemical properties of its silver content.[47] Trade organ *Motion Picture News*, for example, tracks the so-called magic of the silver screen to the "multitudinous processes, repeated tests and unusual cleanliness" that makes the silver in filmic emulsions "the purest that can be obtained."[48] An article for *Educational Film Magazine*, meanwhile, strains even further for scientific credibility. To the accompaniment of a series of glossy photographs, it seeks to account for the wonder of the movies by describing how the "boiling action of nitric acid on ingots of pure silver bullion" delivers an array of "the liquid, brilliant crystals of silver nitrate."[49] If, as Marx puts it, "no chemist has ever discovered exchange-value in a pearl or diamond," these articles sought to do just that, recasting the "social substance" on which moviemaking rests as a strictly "chemical substance" that could be isolated and distilled.[50] By doing so, they sustain a fantasy not only of silver's magical agency but also of the broader "magic" of cinema, erasing the labor that is central to its production and value.

Significantly, this elision of labor, and the fantasy of film magic it supports, is racialized in ways that speak to a resonance between logics of aesthetic transcendence and silver's status as the so-called "white metal." For, while generally expunged from the text, workers *do* appear in *A Movie Trip Through Filmland*; however, these transient or fragmentary glimpses of labor are almost uniformly White. The segment on silver salts, for example, shows a White man opening a cabinet containing a wealth of silver ingots, at which point the film cuts to a close-up image of a White man's hand prodding similar ingots submerged in a vat of nitric acid; as the intertitle explains, "Nitric acid which makes cotton soluble also dissolves silver." Of course, this elision of the labor of non-White, ethnically-othered bodies in the production of silver halide emulsion is, in part, a function of the material realities of the Kodak workforce in the early- to mid-twentieth century. While the company depended on the labor of non-White workers for the extraction and refinement of the silver that fed its emulsions, the staff at Kodak Park in Rochester, New York, was almost exclusively White, Anglo-Saxon, and Protestant.[51] However, by choosing to focus exclusively on the scene of manufacture rather than the scene of extraction, the filmmakers recapitulate Kodak's own elision of non-White labor, underscoring the status of Black and Indigenous labor as what William Brown calls the "structuring Other of white Western modernity."[52] In this context, silver emerges as a luminous surface that both reflects and erases the racialized labor that made it possible, abstracting the work of the non-White bodies that extracted it into pure value. In the process, it helps sustain fantasies of cinema as a space of magical transcendence—a space that, as Richard Dyer has shown, relied on practices such as the "aesthetic technology of light . . . to assume, privilege, and construct an idea of the white person."[53]

III.

Yet if silver was a sentimental commodity that was integral to the early studio-era aesthetic of an (implicitly White) "movie magic," it was also a costly metal that, until relatively recently, served as a formal store of monetary value—a "money commodity" that wore its exchange value very much on the surface.[54] In this sense, it remained tied, inextricably, to what Mary Ann Doane describes as the monetary system's logic of "pure differentiation, quantifiability, and articulation into discrete units."[55] And though never as valuable as gold, silver was expensive. In part, this was thanks to the work of extracting, processing, and shaping the metal. Generally found in alloy or embedded in minerals, silver required extensive smelting and refining, a process largely accomplished, in the interwar years, in the United States.[56] Yet the cost of silver was also subject to more historically proximate pressures in the years immediately following the termination of hostilities in Europe. By the end of 1918, it had increased from US 55c per ounce to a dollar per ounce, in part thanks to the 1918 Pittman Act, which saw the US loan 350 million silver dollars to India to assuage a crisis in the rupee that Britain worried would impair the war effort.[57] While never quite reaching the dizzying heights it had achieved in the aftermath of World War I, the price of silver remained high across the decade; in August 1926, for example, it fetched $8.73 per ounce, in today's US dollars. A number of contemporary pundits, of course, particularly those with industrial interests in stock manufacturing, sought to downplay the cost added to the production of film stock by the ingredient.[58] Yet the 156 tons of silver bullion used each year by leading stock manufacturer Eastman Kodak was no small expense.[59] Each ton of silver would have set Kodak back about $279,360 (again, in today's dollars), meaning that, at a rate of three tons per week, or about 156 tons per year, the company would have been spending approximately US $43,580,160 on silver per annum.

Silver was not the only ingredient in stock that came with a significant price tag.[60] Yet, according to one internal Eastman Kodak document, the price of silver remained "the controlling factor in the cost of Kodak's prime product."[61] Correspondence between Eastman and various Kodak personnel supports this claim. In a 1917 cable to the London office, as silver prices spiked due to wartime shortages, Kodak's founder and CEO George Eastman announced, in terse, telegraphic form, that due to a "big increase [in the] price [of] silver [he] recommend[ed] a price increase."[62] In a 1920 letter to journalist B. C. Forbes, Eastman was again demanding "increases in the selling prices" of film stock "to help meet the still rising cost of silver bullion."[63] And in a 1922 letter to Frank Mattison, the managing director of Kodak's British arm, Eastman was proposing to "take advantage of the evident swings in the level of sterling" by investing in silver stocks.[64] Indeed, the stock manufacturer's frustration with fluctuations in the price of silver was such that in 1918, the year of the Pittman Act, Eastman was considering diversifying into silver mining and refining (just as, in 1930, he would diversify into animal rendering with the establishment of the Eastman Gelatine Corporation).[65] While these proposals never came to fruition, the Kodak Park papers and correspondence between Eastman and the head of the Alaska Mines Corporation suggest that they came remarkably close.[66]

Given Kodak's practice of passing on increases in the cost of silver to its studio clients in Hollywood, it should come as no surprise that Hollywood trade rags were in the habit of keeping a close watch on changes in silver prices across the decade. This habit culminated in reporting around Senator Pittman's proposed, and ultimately realized, tariff hike on silver imported into the US (1930)—a proposal that, according to venues like *Variety*, *Motion Picture News* and *Exhibitors Herald-World*, would likely cost the industry "$10,000,000 if remaining in bill."[67] Yet much as the studios and their trade organs liked to complain about the expense of film stock's raw ingredients, the liability ultimately operated in their favor. As Patricia Zimmerman reminds us, capital-intensive technologies "form a significant barrier to entry" in the industry, helping restrict film production to those with access to ready financing.[68] To the extent that stock itself formed one of the biggest capital outlays in what was already an exceptionally capital-intensive process, it can only have consolidated the dominance of a few major studio players. Whatever the pros and cons of silver's presence in film stock, however, Hollywood's preoccupation with the ingredient suggests that silver must be situated alongside labor and technology as one of the key material resources that the assembly-line practices of the new, "central-producer" mode of production emerged to manage profitably.

And to the extent that this producer-centric mode of production, in turn, served to shape classical Hollywood's sleek, standardized aesthetic economies across the 1920s, the cost of silver must be counted as a factor in the rise of these economies. There is no doubt that the threat of wasted film was a preoccupation among studio executives as they shaped the "quality" multi-reel film into a mass cultural commodity designed to maximize profit by offering spectatorial absorption and narrative integration. In the early 1920s, Warner Brothers—still a minor studio player—began a regime of expansion that involved the improvement of its studio lot and the engagement of new directing, writing, and acting talent. As Sam

Warner himself noted, in coverage of the proposed expansion, savings in film stock were central to the studio's expansionist agenda:

> One of the big factors in the production of a feature is the elimination of waste motion and waste film ... on the whole, the curtailment of wastage of both film and time, and by that I mean closely watching the production and its many phases, will make it possible for exhibitors to book films far cheaper.[69]

Trade journals of the period, meanwhile, are replete with cautions against misuse of film stock during the production process. One instructional article prevailed upon the producer to "observe economy and not waste film, the actor's time or the attention of his audience"; a 1928 industry survey exploring "the possibilities of economy" expressed concern about "large rolls of film [being] thrown into the waste cans because of the fear of running out on an important scene"; while marketing material for the Cinephot "Exposure Meter," an instrument designed to measure exposure on the job, warned readers "[not to] Waste Film and Opportunity."[70] If, as Bordwell et al. have suggested, classical Hollywood cinema's market-driven aesthetic practices received their logic in part from systems designed for efficient and profitable mass production, silver's role in shaping these systems implicates it directly in the rise of the classical Hollywood style.

Silver's presence in film stock helped mold early studio-era Hollywood film aesthetics at the production end, then; but it was also a consideration at the point of post-production. While tales of silver salts being converted back into raw material are often dismissed as apocryphal, the reclamation of silver—whether from the fixing bath after the emulsion had set or by melting finished film stock down afterwards—was standard practice in the 1920s. Even across the early 1920s, most film processing laboratories featured a pair of large tanks for receiving waste "fixing bath" or "hypo"—the exhausted or used solution from the fixing process.[71] Once enough waste fixing bath had been collected, laboratory technicians would use chemical compounds like sodium sulphide to extract the silver in the form of silver sulphide or metal.[72] Investment in this process ramped up after

1925, when leading Kodak chemist K. C. D. Hickman introduced a means of determining the amount of silver in a fixing bath called the "argentometor"; "pil[ing it] . . . in the back of a car," he drove it to Hollywood "and installed [it] in some of the major motion picture studios."[73] Moreover—director Erich von Stroheim's "forty-three cents" jeer aside—the sale of extracted silver could be profitable. By 1921, some studios were recovering anywhere between $500 and $1000 from fixing solutions, scrap paper, and spoiled prints per annum; by 1934, when President Franklin D. Roosevelt's "silver nationalization order" set 500 ounces as the maximum amount of silver that could be held by any one person for industrial purposes, an estimated $200,000 worth of silver was found to be "on hand among th[ose] large studios operating their own laboratories."[74] And evidence suggests that the recovery of silver was seen as a reliable means of offsetting box-office losses.[75] A 1926 edition of *Motion Picture Magazine*, for example, described silver recovery as a process by which the filmmaker could "extract therefrom the silver, in a different form, which the unfortunate producer has failed to get at the box-offices of the country's movie houses, and to melt down the celluloid"—pointing to an established equivalence between box-office revenue and scrap silver yield.[76]

While studio practices organized around the silver reclamation process appear *post hoc* in relation to the aesthetics of the finished filmic commodity, these practices had significant ramifications for the way Hollywood aesthetics have taken shape in historical memory. The well-rehearsed drama of the "mutilation" and subsequent "reconstruction" of the original eight-hour cut of *Greed* (1924) provides a case in point here. As detailed in the introduction to this chapter, when von Stroheim refused to reduce the length of his film further than twenty-four reels, it was not only taken out of his hands and trimmed to just ten reels, but the original "waste footage" was melted down to extract the silver content. This is not, of course, to say that MGM's radical editing process was *motivated by* the desire to extract silver from the stock; on the contrary, it was driven by a concern with the expectations of exhibitors, audiences, and finally, the censorship board.[77] Yet in combination with other examples of the silver recovery process in action, the effective destruction of *Greed*'s negatives has directly shaped our understanding of Hollywood film aesthetics by leaving its mark on the archive. When in later decades *Greed* secured a reputation as a unique masterpiece of "Hollywood naturalism,"[78] efforts to fully reconstruct the forty-two reel original were unsuccessful: the cut footage had been destroyed during the silver reclamation process, and the "restored" *Greed* released by MGM merely combines the surviving footage with some 650 still photographs of the lost scenes in accordance with von Stroheim's original continuity script. While critics and archivists celebrate *Greed* as one of the rare "moments in which the normative humanism of Hollywood [was] penetrated" by alternative narrative possibilities, the actual scope of this experiment in naturalism has been struck from Hollywood's aesthetic record.[79] And silver played no insignificant part in bringing us to this pass.

Silver's presence in photographic film stock was not, of course, inevitable, nor were its presence and effects unmediated by sociopolitical forces. Alternatives to the use of silver salts were available as far back as 1926, when Alfred Weingarten, a professor in Berlin, hit upon a satisfactory substitute.[80] Weingarten's patent for "silverless motion picture positive film" used potassium chromate rather than silver compounds to sensitize the gelatin to light.[81] According to Joe W. Coffman, then Vice-President of early producer of film materials Carpenter-Goldman Laboratories, silverless film had the potential to deliver "a considerable saving in the cost of raw stock."[82] It also offered a number of aesthetic and practical benefits: not only did it "reduce print cost," it also "increase[d] durability of prints; reduce[d] graininess ... [and] minimize[d] distortion."[83] Yet, despite its host of advantages, the technology for silverless film did not gain traction with manufacturers, and would continue to be floated as an as-yet-undeveloped novelty in trade journals until the 1980s.

While we cannot know for certain why "silverless" film was not widely adopted, one explanation is that manufacturers like Eastman Kodak and the emerging DuPont-Pathé resisted the expensive transformations of their supply chains and manufacturing processes that would be required to deliver a new kind of stock.[84] This hypothesis is supported, in part, by the shifting position of the daily trade press on this novel film stock recipe. On August 11, 1926, *Film Daily* ran a short, euphoric note on its front page. Entitled "Silverless film," it cited a "report from Berlin" about the development of a silverless stock, the effect of which was "most satisfactory," and which could result in the "manufacturing cost. ... [being] reduced by fifty percent."[85] The very next day, however, the magazine released a second article entitled "Silver Salts Needed" that backpedaled on the previous day's claims and included derisory quotes from representatives of Eastman Kodak.[86] These criticisms of Weingarten's innovation, meanwhile, were recapitulated in the same paper the day after that, with a second article devoted to its apparent inadequacy.[87] This quickly changing story suggests that some agency—again, most likely, those in the business of manufacturing and marketing motion picture film stock—had intervened to shut down positive publicity for the novel technology.

Whatever the basis of its ongoing use, silver remained a central ingredient in standard filmic emulsions, and, given its expense, it must be numbered among the various capital costs that helped shape the early Hollywood studio system's "central producer" schema and its various aesthetic corollaries. Indeed, while trade journals of the period were conspicuously silent on the aesthetic implications of film stock's silver content, contemporary commentators associated with the thriving 1920s filmic avant-garde, like Jean Epstein and Fernand Léger, elucidated these implications all too clearly. For Epstein and Léger, silver's use as a raw material in motion picture film stock registers only obliquely in what are ultimately allegorical rather than documentary accounts of commercial cinema. However, Epstein and Léger's use of silver in the context of their critiques of the commercial logic of filmmaking supports this article's effort to establish a link between the silver salts in film stock and the rise of a standardized classical Hollywood style. Pioneering experimental filmmaker and theorist Epstein is exemplary here. In his 1922 essay "Langue D'Or," Epstein sought to complicate the "dream[s] of a prodigious universal tongue" that then animated a great deal of commentary on the new medium's aesthetic possibilities. His means of doing so, however, did not involve emphasizing the arbitrariness of the signifier, its contingent relation to the signified. Rather, it involved underscoring the signifier's materiality, and its reliance on precious metals. Film is, according to Epstein,

> A golden language, much more expensive than was silence in a time long ago when speech was silvery. Each celluloid word consumes dollars, marks, francs. And it cannot be pronounced except upon the say-so of bankers, pregnant with capital, after signing contracts in which hundreds of thousands are pledged, exchanged, won, promised, lost, divided, and multiplied. Each word must pay for insurance and customs duty, be amortized and rake in a lot.[88]

While this passage casts the language of cinema as a golden language rather than a silver one, the silver at the end of the first sentence "rubs off," figuratively speaking, on the gold that opens it. And both metals, in turn, are ultimately absorbed into a broader rhetorical agenda—namely, that of setting the weight and grain of film as a medium against the utopian capacities often ascribed to "the movies." Film, Epstein reminds us, is a form of speech in which every utterance "consumes dollars, marks, francs," implying that, far from "free" or universal, it is a language mortgaged to the "say-so of bankers," a language predicated on mercenary calculation. For many theorists, film is a medium appropriated *by* Hollywood capital, especially across the 1920s with the consolidation of the studio system. For Epstein, by contrast, the medium has capital baked into its very essence. In other words, it is the medium's status as a "golden language" that accounts for the marginalization of independent, free-form artistic experimentation and the ascendance of Hollywood's Fordist mode of production across the early twentieth century.

In his 1923 essay "Ballet Méchanique," meanwhile, French painter, filmmaker, and sculptor Léger further unpacks some of the aesthetic implications of photographic film stock's silver content:

> To know how to deal with constraints in the midst of abundance is a rare talent. It's difficult to be rich. The cinema is in danger of dying from it. In its gilded theaters with its silver stars, it doesn't even take the trouble to think up its

own stories; it pirates from the theater, it copies plays. Then you can imagine for yourself that the recruitment of the human material necessary for these enterprises isn't difficult. Anybody will do. I take a well-known play. I add a well-known star. I mix . . .[89]

For Léger, cinema's reliance on this expensive store of value at the level both of exhibition ("gilded theatres") and of production ("silver stars") forces the industry's aesthetic hand in directions most clearly captured by what Horkheimer and Adorno pejoratively call "mass culture"—the standardized products of a benighted "culture industry" in which the commercial imperative of providing "entertainment and relaxation" has overtaken the artistic imperative of "purposiveness without purpose."[90] In keeping with the quantitative logic of the "currency" at its core, then, filmmakers turn to artistic practices that rest on banal, recipe-like formulae ("I take a well-known play, I add a well-known star. I mix"). Yet this mercenary calculus readily devolves into theft and appropriation, or what Léger calls "pirat[ing] or copy[ing]." For both Léger and Epstein, then, film stock's inherent expense—an expense articulated in and through the rubric of precious metal—constrained the emerging industry's stylistic choices, pointing away from oppositional or experimental modes. While, for many theorists, film is either functionally *like* capital (as in Debord or Beller), or was historically appropriated *by* capital, in this vision, thanks to silver, film technology simply *is* capital.[91] Moreover, if this capital is always racial capital—predicated on the conversion of non-White bodies into the spectacle of White cinematic value—the turn to the classical Hollywood style is not only something of a *fait accompli*, but part of the systematic construction of Whiteness.

IV.

The aesthetics of the classical Hollywood narrative film in the early studio era were profoundly contradictory. At a textual level, examples of what Bordwell et al. call Hollywood cinema's "distinct and homogeneous style" are standardized narratives designed to maximize appeal to audiences and to ensure efficiencies of production.⁹² At the level of reception aesthetics, however, these films sustain spectatorial fantasies of transcending market logics—fantasies of "film magic" that elide the social labor of film's production, distribution, and consumption. While the emergence of this distinctive "commodity aesthetic" is conventionally traced to industrial, economic, and cultural developments, I have sought to trace its debts to a more local and more proximate cause: that of the silver content of cellulose nitrate film stock. First, using Marxist theories of the commodity, I unpacked silver's dual politico-material profile, characterizing the soft, lustrous metal as at once a "sentimental commodity" and a "money commodity." Then, I tracked silver's remarkably dual, if complementary, aesthetic effects on both the subjective experience and the objective form of the classical Hollywood cinema across the 1920s. More specifically, I have shown how the silver content in photographic emulsions served at once to reinforce fetishistic hyperbole about a cinematic "magic" untouched by the market, and to constrain film production to observe aesthetic economies that were a direct function of market edicts. In doing so, I hope to have contributed to two lines of inquiry in particular. First, I have sought to complicate standard histories of film aesthetics by ascribing some of the aesthetic characteristics of Hollywood narrative cinema in the early studio era not directly to the force of cultural, industrial, or technological formations, but to a raw geological material in which these forces converge in often surprising ways. Second, I have sought to extend contemporary eco-material approaches to film history by showing that, more than just being significant to industrial, material, and ecological histories of Hollywood, this not-so-humble mineral played a role in molding the classical Hollywood style across the early years of the studio system.

Notes

1. The Margaret Herrick Library, Los Angeles, Erich von Stroheim Papers, box 13, folder 189, "Writings Undated," unpublished autobiographical manuscript "Hollywood—Then and Now (O Tempora, O Mores!)," 132.
2. von Stroheim, quoted in Peter Noble, *Hollywood Scapegoat: The Biography of Erich von Stroheim* (London: Fortune Press, 1950), 52.

3. For this reading of the film's production history, see Ryan Bishop and Sean Cubitt, "Anti-Humanist Narratives: *Greed* and *Source Code*," *Screen* 58, no. 1 (2017): 1–17; Jared Gardner, "What Blood Will Tell: Hereditary Determinism in *McTeague* and *Greed*," *Texas Studies in Literature and Language* 36, no. 1 (1994): 51–74; Lea Jacobs, *The Decline of Sentiment: American Film in the 1920s* (Berkeley: University of California Press, 2009); Fredric Jameson, "*The Shining*," *Social Text* 4 (1981): 114; Richard Koszarski, *Von: The Life and Films of Erich von Stroheim* (New York: Limelight Press, 2001). For examples of this narrative more generally, see David Bordwell, Janet Staiger, and Kristin Thompson, *The Classical Hollywood Cinema: Film Style and Mode of Production to 1960* (New York: Routledge, 2003); Douglas Gomery, *Hollywood Studio System: A History* (London: Bloomsbury Academic, 2005); Thomas Schatz, *The Genius of the System: Hollywood Filmmaking in the Studio Era* (New York: Henry Holt and Company, 2015).
4. Bordwell et al., *The Classical Hollywood Cinema*.
5. Sianne Ngai, *Our Aesthetic Categories: Zany, Cute, Interesting* (Cambridge, MA: Harvard University Press, 2012), 29.
6. Karl Marx, *Capital: A Critique of Political Economy, Vol. I*, trans. Ben Fowkes, ed. Ernest Mandel (London: Penguin Books, 1999), 169. My italics.
7. Charlie Keil and Shelley Stamp, *American Cinema's Transitional Era: Audiences, Institutions, Practices* (Berkeley, CA: University of California Press, 2004).
8. In other words, it combined a fetishistic or "magical" allure that seemed to radiate from the cinematic object itself with standardized narrative and formal economies that were clearly shaped by the cinematic object's conditions of production, circulation, and consumption. Bordwell et al., *The Classical Hollywood Cinema*; Marx, *Capital*, 169.
9. Tom Gunning "Modernity and Cinema: A Culture of Shocks and Flows," in Murray Pomerance, ed., *Cinema and Modernity* (New Jersey: Rutgers University Press, 2005), 297–315; Gomery, *The Hollywood Studio System*; Bordwell et al., *The Classical Hollywood Cinema*, 263–284.
10. Marx, *Capital*, 169.
11. Michael Heinrich, *An Introduction to the Three Volumes of Karl Marx's Capital* (New York: NYU Press, 2012), 67.
12. Jane Bennett, *Vibrant Matter: A Political Ecology of Things* (Durham NC: Duke University Press, 2012), 28.
13. Dipesh Chakrabarty, "The Climate of History: Four Theses," *Critical Inquiry* 35, no. 2 (2009): 197–222. For an exposition of this model of matter as conjunction of the physical, the political, the discursive, and the industrial, see Bennett, *Vibrant Matter*.
14. Bruno Latour, *We Have Never Been Modern* (Cambridge, MA: Harvard University Press, 2012), 2–3, 6.

15. Douglas Gomery, "The Hollywood Studio System," in *The Oxford History of World Cinema*, ed. Geoffrey Nowell-Smith (Oxford: Oxford University Press, 2005), 43–53; Laura Mulvey, *Fetishism and Curiosity* (Bloomington, IN: Indiana University Press, 2006), 8; Wasko, *Movies and Money*, 21.
16. For example, through the use of a goal-oriented protagonist, a rising curve of action and a naturalistic "continuity" system of editing (Bordwell et al., *Classical Hollywood Cinema*, 3–84; Gomery, *The Hollywood Studio System*; Schatz, *The Genius of the System*).
17. R. Herring, "A New Cinema, Magic and the Avant-Garde," *Close Up* 4, no. 4 (1929): 48.
18. Matthew Solomon, *Disappearing Tricks: Silent Film, Houdini, and the New Magic of the Twentieth Century* (Chicago: University of Illinois Press, 2010), 5. See also Karen Beckman, *Vanishing Women: Magic, Film, and Feminism* (Durham, NC: Duke University Press, 2003); Colin Williamson, *Hidden in Plain Sight: An Archaeology of Magic and the Cinema* (New Brunswick: Rutgers University Press, 2015). A 1922 article in *Photoplay* entitled "A Romantic History of the Motion Picture," for example, opens with an extended paean to the "magic" of the cinema as a "world of make-believe, a magic land of Far and Away, where impossible hopes are broken and improbable dreams come true" (Terry Ramsaye, "The Romantic History of the Motion Picture," *Photoplay* 21, no. 5 [1922]: 20).
19. Theodor W. Adorno and Max Horkheimer, *Dialectic of Enlightenment* (London: Verso, 1997), 135.
20. Robert Beverley Ray, *How a Film Theory Got Lost and Other Mysteries in Cultural Studies* (Bloomington: Indiana University Press, 2001), 2.
21. William L. Silber, *The Story of Silver: How the White Metal Shaped America and the Modern World* (New Jersey: Princeton University Press, 2019), 3.
22. Karl Marx, *Capital: A Critique of Political Economy, Vol I*, trans. Ben Fowkes, ed. Ernest Mandel (London: Penguin Books, 1999), 169.
23. Lynn Festa, *Sentimental Figures of Empire in Eighteenth Century Britain and France* (Baltimore, MA: Johns Hopkins University Press, 2006), 115.
24. Esther Forbes, *Paul Revere and the World He Lived in* (Boston: Houghton Mifflin Harcourt, 1942), 67.
25. On the "whiteness" of silver, see "Rise of Eastman Kodak Company Constitutes Industrial Romance," *The Moving Picture World*, August 16, 1919, 960; "Kodak Film in the Making," *Educational Film Magazine* 1, no. 6 (1919): 24; "Sidelights on Manufacture of Motion Picture Film," *Motion Picture News*, July 13, 1918, 272. Thanks to Kirsty Dootson for these references.
26. Kirsty Dootson, "Celluloid Skin," in *Film Stock*, eds. Alice Lovejoy, Kirsty Dootson, and Pansy Duncan (Minneapolis: Minnesota University Press, forthcoming). For more on this topic, see Monica Bravo, "Mercury Rising: US–Mexican Conflict in Alexander Edouart's Blessing of the Enrequita Mine,"

Art History 46, no. 3 (2023): 540–567; Siobhan Angus, *Camera Geologica: An Elemental History of Photography* (Durham, NC: Duke University Press, 2023).
27. Lynn Dumenil and Eric Foner, *The Modern Temper: American Culture and Society in the 1920s* (London: Macmillan, 1995).
28. Festa, *Sentimental Figures*, 69; Beth Carver Wees and Medill Higgins Harvey, *Early American Silver in The Metropolitan Museum of Art* (New York: Metropolitan Museum of Art, 2013), 120.
29. Beth Carver Wees and Medill Higgins Harvey, *Early American Silver in The Metropolitan Museum of Art* (New York: Metropolitan Museum of Art, 2013), 120.
30. Advertisement, *Motion Pictures News* April 22, 1922, 2268; "3 Bad Men Will Carry Forward Work of Thrilling Film Fans," *Fox Folks* 5, no 8 (1923): 15; "Production Highlights," *Exhibitors' Trade Review*, 25 April, 1925, 33. Interestingly, the fact that film was widely perceived as a "silver" medium barely warrants a mention in recent revisionist histories of film color. See, for example, Joshua Yumibe, *Moving Color: Early Film, Mass Culture, Modernism* (New Jersey: Rutgers University Press, 2012), 4; Richard Misek, *Chromatic Cinema: A History of Screen Colour* (Malden, MA: Wiley-Blackwell, 2010), 14.
31. John L. Cass, "Painting the Silver Sheet," *Motion Picture Projectionist*, February 1932, 8.
32. John Scotland, *The Talkies* (London: C. Lockwood and Son, 1930), 171; Herbert C. McKay, *Handbook of Motion Picture Photography* (London: Falk Publishing Company, 1927), 243.
33. H. T. Cowling, "India's New Magic," *International Photographer*, May 1929, 14–15.
34. Terry Ramsaye, "Chemists Speed Printing Time of News Pictures in Colour," *Pathé Sun*, 5 April 1930, 10.
35. Dwight R. Furness, "Some Secrets of Screen Magic," *Amateur Movie Makers*, 15 January 1927, 26.
36. Franklin Courtney Ellis, "Motion Picture Film in the Making, Part II," *Motion Picture Projectionist*, June 1932, 12.
37. Jane Bennett, *The Enchantment of Modern Life* (New Jersey: Princeton University Press, 2000), 113.
38. "Eastman Industrial Takes Public through Big Film Plant," *Exhibitors Herald*, 11 February (1922): 50.
39. Marx, *Capital*, 279–80.
40. Sharon Corwin, "Picturing Efficiency," *Representations* 94 (2004): 147; "Eastman Industrial Takes Public through Big Film Plant," 50.
41. Sharon Corwin, "Picturing Efficiency," *Representations* 94 (2004): 147; "Eastman Industrial Takes Public through Big Film Plant," 50.

42. The three-part series on raw stock production by Franklin Ellis in *Motion Picture Projectionist* cited above also represents silver bullion as the subject rather than the object of manufacturing processes in what the author tellingly calls the industry's "modern alchemy": There, on our right, is a building in which silver ... *is turning* into ... motion picture film ..."; "four tons a week [of silver] ... *passes* [sic] through the storage safe" (Franklin Courtney Ellis, "Motion Picture Film in the Making, Part I," *Motion Picture Projectionist*, May [1932], 7). When the author mentions workers at all, they are magicians rather than laborers, "witches" who "conjure up several hundred thousand miles of magical ribbon every year [without] conical caps [or] broomsticks" (Ellis, "Motion Picture Film in the Making, Part I," 6).
43. Salomé Aguilera Skvirsky, *The Process Genre: Cinema and the Aesthetic of Labour* (Durham, NC: Duke University Press, 2020), 117.
44. Skvirsky, *The Process Genre*, 136, 141.
45. Tom Gunning, "Crazy Machines in the Garden of Forking Paths," in *Classical Hollywood* Comedy, eds. Kristine Brunovska Karnick and Henry Jenkins (New York, NY: Routledge, 1998); Neil Harris, *Humbug: The Art of T. Barnum* (Chicago: Chicago University Press, 1973), 57; Paul Young, "Media on Display: A Telegraphic History of Early American Cinema," in *New Media: 1740–1915*, eds. Lisa Gitelman and Geoffrey B. Pingree (Cambridge, MA: MIT Press, 2003), 229–264.
46. Harris, *Humbug*, 57.
47. Marx, *Capital*, 165.
48. "Sidelights on Manufacture of Motion Picture Film," *Motion Picture News*, July 13, 1918, 271, 270.
49. Leona Block, "Movie Trip through Filmland," *Educational Film Magazine* 8, no. 6 (1922): 16.
50. Marx, *Capital*, 177, 128, 177.
51. Sanford N. Jacoby, *Modern Manors: Welfare Capitalism Since the New Deal* (Princeton, NJ: Princeton University Press, 1998), 57.
52. William Brown, *Navigating from the White Anthropocene to the Black Cthulucene* (Winchester, UK: Zero Books, 2023), 54.
53. Richard Dyer, *White: Essays on Race and Culture* (New York: Routledge, 2006), 84.
54. A. Nelson, "Marx's Theory of the Money Commodity," *History of Economics Review* 33, no. 1 (2001): 45.
55. Mary Ann Doane, *The Emergence of Cinematic Time: Modernity, Contingency, the Archive* (Cambridge MA: Harvard University Press), 8.
56. Silber, *The Story of Silver*, 43.
57. G. F. Shirras, "Some Effects of the War on Gold and Silver," *Journal of the Royal Statistical Society* 83, no. 4 (1920): 572–627.
58. "Silver Salts Needed," *Film Daily*, August 12, 1926, 6.

59. G. A. Blair, "The Development of the Motion Picture Raw Film Industry," *Annals of the American Academy of Political and Social Science* 128, no. 1 (1926): 50–53.
60. "The Story of Kodak," 22.
61. KHC, box 39, folder 11, "A Kind of Magic," 26.
62. George Eastman House, Rochester, George Eastman Legacy Collection (Henceforth GELC), George Eastman outgoing correspondence, September 13, 1917.
63. GELC, George Eastman outgoing correspondence, June 10, 1920.
64. GELC, George Eastman outgoing correspondence, March 3, 1920.
65. KHC, box 39, folder 11, "Gelatin is Simple Stuff," 1.
66. KHC, box 39, folder 11, "A Kind of Magic," 26; GELC, George Eastman outgoing correspondence, June 29, 1918.
67. Anonymous, "Tariff on Silver," *Variety*, April 2, 1930, 11. See also Francis L. Burt, "Proposed Silver Duty Saddles 10 Millions Cost on Film Trade," *Exhibitor's Herald-World*, March 29, 1930, 21.
68. Patricia Zimmermann, *Reel Families: A Social History of Amateur Film* (Bloomington: Indiana University Press, 1995), 3.
69. "Warners Enlarge Studio for Increased Production Schedule," *Moving Picture World*, March, 1923, 198.
70. R. W. Winton, "Why Films Go Wrong," *Movie Makers* May 1929, 287–289; L. Physioc, "Economy of Production," *American Cinematographer* 8, no. 12 (1928): 9–10; Cinephot advertisement, *Movie Makers*, March 1929, 183.
71. The "fixing" process was the process used to remove unexposed and undeveloped silver halide crystals from the film emulsion to make the image stable and insensitive to light.
72. Hickman and Hyndman, "Automatic Silver Recovery from Hypo," *Transactions of the Society of Motion Picture Engineers* 11, no. 32 (1927): 699.
73. K. H. C., Box 96, Folder 11, "K. C. D. Hickman and Distillation Products," 5.
74. Pell Mitchell, "Cameraman's Question Box," *Exhibitor's Trade Review*s 10, no. 21 (1921): 1479; "Silver Order No Bar to Industrial Users," *Motion Picture Herald*, August 18, 1934, 10. Industrial users of silver, like Kodak, were exceptions to this edict.
75. I. Crabtree and J. F. Ross, "Silver Recovery from Exhausted Fixing Bath," *Transactions of the Society of Motion Picture Engineers*, May 1926, 71.
76. B. Ennis, "The Place of Missing Films," *Motion Picture Magazine* 31, no. 5 (1926): 22, 98.
77. Koszarski, *Von*, 168.
78. Lea Jacobs, *The Decline of Sentiment: American Film in the 1920s* (Berkeley: University of California Press, 2009), 25.
79. Bishop and Cubitt, "Anti-Humanist Narratives," 1.
80. Joe W. Coffman, "Silverless Motion Picture Positive Film," in *Transactions of the Society of Motion Picture Engineers* 12, no. 34 (1928): 370.

96 The Natural History of Film Form

81. Coffman, "Silverless Motion Picture Positive Film," 370.
82. Coffman, "Silverless Motion Picture Positive Film," 370.
83. Coffman, "Silverless Motion Picture Positive Film," 379, 381.
84. This resistance on the part of film manufacturers to industrial change had precedents, for example, in Kodak's resistance to the development of panchromatic film stock due to "its problematic production" (Luci Marzola, "Better Pictures through Chemistry: DuPont and the Fight for the Hollywood Film Stock Market," *The Velvet Light Trap*, no. 76 [2015]: 18).
85. "Silverless Film," *The Film Daily*, August 11, 1926, 1.
86. "Silver Salts Needed," *Film Daily*, August 12, 1926, 6.
87. "Speed Essential," *Film Daily*, August 13, 1926, 1, 5.
88. Jean Epstein, "Langue D'Or," in *Jean Epstein: Critical Essays and New Translations*, eds. Sarah Keller and Jason N. Paul (Amsterdam: Amsterdam University Press, 2012), 297.
89. Fernand Léger, "Ballet Mecanique," in *Functions of Painting*, ed. Edward F. Fry, trans. Alexandra Anderson (New York: Viking Press, 1973), 50.
90. Adorno and Horkheimer, *Dialectic of Enlightenment*, 128.
91. Guy Debord, *Society of the Spectacle* (London: Bread and Circuses Publishing, N.D.), 8; Jonathan Beller, *The Cinematic Mode of Production: Attention Economy and the Society of the Spectacle* (Lebanon, NH: University Press of New England, 2006), 45, 46.
92. Bordwell, Staiger, and Thompson, *The Classical Hollywood Cinema*, 3.

Conclusion: Lithium Aesthetics

A Natural History of Film Form is an eco-materialist history of film aesthetics. It traces the entanglements between celluloid's bio- and geophysical ingredients on the one hand, and some dominant aesthetic regimes in Euro-American cinema's extended "early" period on the other. As I have shown, even prior to their application to the moving image medium, these nature/culture "hybrids" had acquired a unique "politico-material" profile, meaning that they were embedded in, and had come to embody, some of modern industrial capitalism's central tensions. This book has argued that the "politico-material" agency of each raw material helped shape, and, in the process, code, early cinema's signature aesthetic regimes: the "transformation view," a sub-genre of trick film oriented around scenes of magical metamorphosis and popular across the early novelty period (1895–1907); the early "popular science" film, which flourished during cinema's transitional years (1907–1914); and the early Classical Hollywood style as it flourished in the incipient studio era (1914–1925). As this suggests, this book takes aim at film studies' idealizing and dematerializing tendency to extract the filmic image from its eco-material context. Throughout, I have embedded the cinematic image in what Jussi Parikka calls "dirty matter" in an effort to reconnect the images we see, the sounds we hear and the things we feel with the geo- and biophysical ingredients that sustain these aesthetic experiences.[1]

Yet if this book involves an anti-idealizing gesture, it also involves an anti-anthropocentric one. In other words, it queries film studies' anthropocentric tendency to represent the history of film aesthetics almost exclusively as a history of human activity. The locus classicus of this mode of thinking is the "auteur theory" that dominated film theory and criticism in the formative decades of the '50s and '60s and that ascribed the evolution of film aesthetics to the visionary activity of genius auteurs. Yet, from revitalized apparatus theories to technological histories of cinema, industry studies, and new formalisms, many contemporary critical frameworks center the role of human beings and human societies in shaping film aesthetics and culture. Of course, I don't intend to suggest that the three ingredients at the heart of *The Natural History of Film Form* exist beyond the reach of human culture and industry. On the contrary, they are by-products of sophisticated extraction and refinement processes driven by human enterprise in the context of industrial capitalism. The production of silver, which is often found in alloy with other metals, requires mining and refining; as the first synthetic plastic, celluloid depends on an industrial synthesis of nitrocellulose and camphor; similarly, deriving gelatin from the collagen taken from animal body parts involves a multistage process of hydrolosis, filtration, clarification, evaporation, drying, and sifting. Yet the ingredients in question also exceed the processes that bring them into existence as industrial commodities. Gelatin, even after processing, remains vulnerable to bacterial infection; silver is difficult to find and extract; and celluloid is as worryingly explosive as it is ideally malleable. These are "hybrid" materials, uniquely modern fusions of "natural" and "human" history, and thus never entirely containable within the sphere of human activity and influence.

In advancing this argument, this book has focused on silver, gelatin, and celluloid as film stock's primary ingredients, yet there are other minerals that have fed into that film stock and that would reward further research. As Wolfgang Berg has noted, gold was also used in microscopic quantities in filmic emulsions to increase their sensitivity up to two to three times, whether by stabilizing the "small growing silver centre at a stage when it might otherwise be subject to regression," or by ensuring that even very small silver centers are available for development.[2] In 1998, Eastman Kodak, via inventors Kenneth Lushington and Henry J. Gysling, filed a patent with the

US patent office that involved the addition of a "gold compound" to the silver halide emulsion.[3] Moving beyond film stock, we might consider the extent to which other natural resources, from rain to fossil fuels to sunlight, have shaped cinema's changing sensory regimes. In his excellent analysis of *Singin' in the Rain* (Donen/Kelly, 1952), for example, Hunter Vaughan explores the reliance of the film's titular rain-soaked dance sequence on the use of vast quantities of water, a resource-intensive spectacle that embodies the extravagant use of natural resources in mid-twentieth-century Hollywood filmmaking.[4] Similarly, Nadia Bozak has explored the role of the "economics of sunlight" in shaping the geographic form of American cinema, with evolving filmmaking technologies and production contexts prompting producers alternately to exploit and to block out available sunlight.[5]

The question, of course, is how claims about film stock's specific role in this drama apply today—a moment in which celluloid has been phased out as an industrial standard, and in which film production, storage, distribution, and consumption rely heavily on digital technologies. There are two potential answers to this question. The first is that many of the aesthetic logics for which this book provides speculative "origin stories" still have significant purchase. To say that these aesthetic logics can be traced, in part, to the animal, vegetable, and mineral ingredients of cellulose nitrate film stock is not to say that they lose their power the moment this technology is rolled back. The trick film and its descendants continue to entertain and amuse us, from Hollywood stunt work to the TikTok #floatingbodyparts dance challenge. Gelatin, similarly, plays no role in film production today, but most film historical scholarship has an oddly aseptic understanding of a technology that was in fact heavily dependent on the collagen of dead animals, testifying to gelatin's politico-material status as "animal no more." Finally, the legacy of silver's presence in film stock lives on in the abiding vision of Hollywood cinema as both commodity and magic that silver helped to seed.

The second answer to the question, however, is that there is scope to apply some of the approaches set out in this book to the raw ingredients of contemporary digital film production technology.

Yes, making connections between the eco-material and aesthetic registers is more straightforward in the context of early film production culture, which was marked by an exceptional degree of proximity between film direction and film processing. But these connections retain their relevance in the context of digital aesthetics, as attested by critical accounts of the ways in which, say, petroleum has shaped contemporary culture.[6]

How, then, might we begin to trace similar links in the context of digital film production? It is now a critical commonplace to note the extent to which, while shaped by fantasies of immateriality, digital film culture is underpinned by "new flows of resources."[7] Among the materials anchoring this new economy is lithium, a very soft silvery-white metal that is central to the re-chargeable "lithium ion" batteries that have been used, since the early 2000s, to power digital cameras on most film sets with ties to affluent nations.[8] Today, many Western automobile executives are bypassing traditional supply chains and investing billions directly in mining deals across South America's resource-rich "lithium triangle" of Argentina, Chile, and Bolivia. Like gelatin, silver, and cellulose, lithium, often known as white gold, has a clear politico-material profile as a kind of futuristic metal—"the gold of the twenty first century," light, easy, and cheap to extract.[9] In *The Beauty of Chemistry*, Philip Ball identifies lithium as a "lightweight metal," providing the same or greater energy at less than half the weight and size of other battery chemistry.[10] Lithium batteries are also more efficient; whereas 95 per cent or more of the energy stored in a lithium-ion battery is usable, in the case of lead acid batteries this is closer to 80 to 85 per cent. Finally, lithium charges at a very high speed, thereby minimizing charging downtime.

The predominance of lithium batteries in film production has, arguably, helped shape our understanding of the aesthetic possibilities of the medium. Is it an accident, for example, that the increasingly central role in film production technologies of this quick-charging, lightweight and efficient metal corresponds with the rise of a form of cinema in which speed is an aesthetic watchword? Since the early 2000s, critics and film scholars have noted the emergence of what Tina Kendall identifies as a new cinema of speed, and that David

Bordwell, Peter Wollen, and Steven Shaviro have described under the rubrics of "intensified continuity," "post-continuity," or "accelerationist aesthetics," respectively.[11] Crystallized in these accounts is a reference to the hyperkinetic, adrenaline-charged style embraced by blockbuster films across the twenty-first century, including franchises such as *Transformers* (Michael Bay, 2007–2014), *Bourne* (Doug Liman, Paul Greengrass, and Tony Gilroy, 2002–2012), *The Avengers* (Joss Whedon, Anthony Russo, and Joe Russo, 2012–2023), and *Fast & Furious* (Rob Cohen, John Singleton, Justin Lin, James Wan, F. Gary Grey, Philip Atwell, Rob Cohen, Vin Diesel, and Louis Leterrier, 2001–2023). What sets these blockbuster franchises apart from earlier forms of narrative cinema is that they emphasize pace and energy to a degree that, as Lutz Koepnick notes, is often understood as a threat to narrative and spatio-temporal legibility.[12] While I am not in a position to make clear causal claims about the relationship between recent formal developments in Hollywood filmmaking and shifts in the geological ingredients feeding filmmaking technology, these correspondences provide rich food for reflection. My hope is that this book has provided some of the theoretical and methodological infrastructure necessary to sustain this reflection.

Notes

1. Jussi Parikka, "New Materialism as Media Theory: Medianatures and Dirty Matter," *Communication and Critical/Cultural Studies* 9, no. 1 (2012): 95–100.
2. Wolfgang F. Berg, "Gold Sensitization in Photography," *Gold Bulletin* 12, no. 3 (1979): 98.
3. https://patents.google.com/patent/US5759761A/en
4. Hunter Vaughan, "500,000 Kilowatts of Stardust," *Sustainable Media*, eds. Janet Walker and Nicole Starosielski, 23–37 (New York, NY: Routledge, 2016).
5. Nadia Bozak, *The Cinematic Footprint: Lights, Camera, Natural Resources* (New Brunswick: Rutgers University Press, 2011), 32.
6. Sheena Wilson, Imre Szeman and Adam Carlson, "On Petrocultures: Or, Why We Need to Understand Oil to Understand Everything Else," in *Petrocultures: Oil, Politics, Culture*, eds. Sheena Wilson, Adam Carlson, and Imre Szeman (Montreal: McGill-Queen's Press-MQUP).

7. Hunter Vaughan, *Hollywood's Dirtiest Secret: The Hidden Environmental Costs of the Movies* (New York: Columbia University Press, 2019), 138.
8. Felix M. Dorn and Fernando Ruiz Peyré, "Lithium as a Strategic Resource: Geopolitics, Industrialization, and Mining in Argentina," *Journal of Latin American Geography* 19, no. 4 (2020): 68–90.
9. Anlauf, quoted in Dorn and Peyré, "Lithium as a Strategic Resource," 68.
10. Philip Ball, *The Beauty of Chemistry* (Cambridge: MIT Press, 2021), 225.
11. Tina Kendall, "Staying On, or Getting Off (the Bus): Approaching Speed in Cinema and Media Studies," *Cinema Journal* 55, no. 2 (2016): 112–118; Karen Beckman, *Crash: Cinema and the Politics of Speed and Stasis* (Duke University Press, 2010); David Bordwell, "Intensified Continuity in American Film," *Film Quarterly* 55, no. 3 (Spring 2002): 16–28; Steven Shaviro, *Post-Cinematic Affect* (Winchester, UK: Zero Books, 2010); Steven Shaviro, "Accelerationist Aesthetics: Necessary Inefficiency in Times of Real Subsumption," *e-flux journal* 46 (2013): http://www.e-flux.com/journal/accelerationist-aesthetics-necessary-inefficiency-in-times-of-real-subsumption/; Peter Wollen, "Speed and the Cinema," *New Left Review* 16 (2002): 105.
12. Lutz Koepnick, *On Slowness: Toward an Aesthetic of the Contemporary* (New York: Columbia University Press, 2014), 153.

Bibliography

Abel, Richard. *The Ciné Goes to Town: French Cinema, 1896-1914*. Berkeley: University of California Press, 1998.
Adorno, Theodor W. and Max Horkheimer. *Dialectic of Enlightenment*. London: Verso, 1997.
Alaimo, Stacy. *Exposed: Environmental Politics and Pleasure in Posthuman Times*. Minneapolis: Minnesota University Press, 2016.
Althusser, Louis, Etienne Balibar, Roger Establet, Pierre Machery, and Jacques Ranciere. *Reading Capital*, translated by Ben Brewster and David Bernbach. London: Verso, 2016.
Angus, Siobhan. *Camera Geologica: An Elemental History of Photography*. Durham, NC: Duke University Press, 2023.
Arabindan-Kesson, Anna. *Black Bodies, White Gold: Art, Cotton, and Commerce in the Atlantic World*. Durham, NC: Duke University Press, 2021.
Ball, Philip. *The Beauty of Chemistry*. Cambridge: MIT Press, 2021.
Barad, Karen. *Meeting the Universe Halfway: Quantum Physics and the Entanglement of Matter and Meaning*. Durham, NC: Duke University Press, 2007.
Barnes, John. *The Beginnings of the Cinema in England, 1894-1901: 1900*. Exeter: Exeter University Press, 1997.
Bazin, Andre and Hugh Gray. "Ontology of the Photographic Image." *Film Quarterly* 13, no 4 (Summer, 1960): 4–9.
Beckman, Karen. *Vanishing Women: Magic, Film, and Feminism*. Durham, NC: Duke University Press, 2003.
Beller, Jonathan. *The Cinematic Mode of Production: Attention Economy and the Society of the Spectacle*. Lebanon, NH: University Press of New England, 2006.
Benjamin, Walter. *The Work of Art in the Age of Its Technological Reproducibility, and Other Writings on Media*. Cambridge, MA: Harvard University Press, 2008.
Bennett, Jane. *The Enchantment of Modern Life*. New Jersey: Princeton University Press, 2000.

Bennett, Jane. *Vibrant Matter: A Political Ecology of Things*. Durham, NC: Duke University Press, 2010.
Berg, Wolfgang F. "Gold Sensitization in Photography." *Gold Bulletin* 12, no. 3 (1979): 97–98.
Biesen, Sheri. *Blackout: World War II and the Origins of Film Noir*. Baltimore: JHU Press, 2005.
Bishop, Ryan and Sean Cubitt. "Anti-Humanist Narratives: *Greed* and *Source Code*." *Screen* 58, no. 1 (2017): 1–17.
Blair, G. A. "The Development of the Motion Picture Raw Film Industry." *Annals of the American Academy of Political and Social Science* 128, no. 1 (1926): 50–53.
Boetzkes, Amanda. "Plastic Vision and the Sight of Petroculture." In *Petrocultures: Oil, Politics, Culture*, edited by Sheena Wilson, Adam Carlson, and Imre Szeman. McGill-Queen's Press-MQUP, 2017.
Bogost, Ian. *Alien Phenomenology, or, What It's Like To Be a Thing*. Minneapolis: University Of Minnesota Press, 2012.
Bordwell, David. "Intensified Continuity in American Film." *Film Quarterly* 55, no. 3 (2002): 16–28.
Bordwell, David, Janet Staiger, and Kristin Thompson. *The Classical Hollywood Cinema: Film Style and Mode of Production to 1960*. New York: Routledge, 2003.
Bozak, Nadia. *The Cinematic Footprint: Lights, Camera, Natural Resources*. New Jersey: Rutgers University Press, 2011.
Braidotti, Rosi. *The Posthuman*. Malden, MA: Polity Press, 2013.
Bravo, Monica. "Mercury Rising: US–Mexican Conflict in Alexander Edouart's Blessing of the Enrequita Mine." *Art History* 46, no. 3 (2023): 540–567.
Brown, Bill. "Materiality." In *Critical Terms for Media Studies*, edited by W. J. T. Mitchell and Mark B. N. Hansen. Chicago: University of Chicago Press, 2010.
Brown, Simon. *Cecil Hepworth and the Rise of the British Film Industry 1899–1911*. Exeter: Exeter University Press, 2016.
Brown, William. *Navigating from the White Anthropocene to the Black Cthulucene*. Winchester, UK: Zero Books, 2023.
Brown, William and David H. Fleming. *The Squid Cinema from Hell: Kinoteuthis Infernalis and the Emergence of Chthulumedia*. Edinburgh: Edinburgh University Press, 2020.
Bruno, Giuliana. *Surface: Matters of Aesthetics, Materiality, and Media*. Chicago: Chicago University Press, 2014.
Buell, Frederick. "A Short History of Oil Cultures: or, the Marriage of Catastrophe and Exuberance." *Journal of American Studies* 46, no. 2 (2012): 273–293.
Cahill, James Leo. "Cinema's Natural History." *Journal of Cinema and Media Studies* 58, no. 2 (2019): 152–257.
Chakrabarty, Dipesh. "The Climate of History: Four Theses." *Critical Inquiry* 35, no. 2 (2009): 197–222.

Chanan, Michael. *The Dream that Kicks: The Prehistory and Early Years of the Cinema in Britain*. London: Routledge, 1996.
Charles Urban Trading Co. Ltd. Catalogue, 1903. London: Charles Urban, 1903.
Charney, Leo and Vanessa R. Schwartz, eds. *Cinema and the Invention of Modern Life*. Berkeley: University of California Press, 1995.
Christie, Ian. "Time Regained: The Complex Magic of Reverse Motion." In *Projected Shadows: Psychoanalytic Reflections on the Representation of Loss in European Cinema*, edited by Andrea Sabbadini. London: Routledge, 2007.
Coffman, Joe W. "Silverless Motion Picture Positive Film." *Transactions of the Society of Motion Picture Engineers* 12, no. 34 (1928): 379–381.
Comandon, Jean. "Biological Physics: Cinematography, with the Ultra-Microscope of Microbes, Living Things and Moving Particles." In *Comptes Rendes Hebdomadaires des seances*, 1909 939.
Comandon, Jean. "Le Cinematographie et les Sciences de la Nature." In *Le Cinema, des origines a nos jours*, edited by Henri Fescourt. Paris: Editions du Cygne, 1932.
Connor, Steven. *The Matter of Air: Science and Art of the Ethereal*. London: Reaktion Books, 2010.
Corwin, Sharon. "Picturing Efficiency." *Representations* 94 (2004): 139–165.
Cowling, H. T. "India's New Magic." *International Photographer*, May 1929, 14–15.
Crabtree, J. I. and J. F. Ross. "Silver Recovery from Exhausted Fixing Bath." *Transactions of the Society of Motion Picture Engineers*, May 1926, 70–84.
Crary, Jonathan. *Techniques of the Observer: On Vision and Modernity in the Nineteenth Century*. Cambridge, MA: MIT Press, 1992.
Cubitt, Sean. *Finite Media: Environmental Implications of Digital Technologies*. Durham, NC: Duke University Press, 2016.
Daston, Lorraine and Peter Galison. "The Image of Objectivity." *Representations* 40 (1992): 81–128.
De Clerck, Elke and Paul De Vos. "Study of the Bacterial Load in a Gelatine Production Process Focussed on Bacillus and Related Endosporeforming General." *Systematic and Applied Microbiology* 25, no. 4 (2002): 611–617.
Debord, Guy. *Society of the Spectacle*. London: Bread and Circuses Publishing, N.D.
Dickson, William Kennedy-Laurie and Antonia Dickson. *History of the Kinetograph, Kinetoscope, and Kinetophonograph*. New York: Albert Bunn, 1895.
Doane, Mary Ann. *The Emergence of Cinematic Time*. Cambridge, MA: Harvard University Press, 2002.
Dootson, Kirsty. "Celluloid Skin." In *Film Stock*, edited by Alice Lovejoy, Kirsty Dootson, and Pansy Duncan. Minneapolis: Minnesota University Press, forthcoming.
Dorn, Felix M. and Fernando Ruiz Peyré. "Lithium as a Strategic Resource: Geopolitics, Industrialization, and Mining in Argentina." *Journal of Latin American Geography* 19, no. 4 (2020): 68–90.

Dumenil, Lynn and Eric Foner. *The Modern Temper: American Culture and Society in the 1920s*. London: Macmillan, 1995.
Duncan, Pansy. "'Journeys of Adventure among Its Far-Flung Debris': Three Theories of the Blockbuster Explosion Spectacle." *JCMS: Journal of Cinema and Media Studies* 59, no. 2 (2020): 1–22.
Dundon, Merle L. and J. I. Crabtree. "Investigations on Photographic Developers: Sulphide Fog by Bacteria in Motion Picture Developers." *Transactions of Society of Motion Picture Engineers*, November 1924, 24–35.
Dyer, Richard. *White: Essays on Race and Culture*. New York: Routledge, 2006.
Eisenstein, Sergei. *Eisenstein on Disney*, edited by Jay Leyda, translated by Alan Upchurch. London: Methuen, 1988.
Ellis, Franklin Courtney. "Motion Picture Film in the Making, Part II." *Motion Picture Projectionist*, June 1932, 12–14.
Elsaesser, Thomas. "The New Film History as Media Archaeology." *Cinémas* 14, no. 2–3 (2004): 75–117.
Engels, Fredrich and Karl Marx. "Manifesto of the Communist Party." In Karl Marx, *The Revolutions of 1848*. London: Pelican Marx Library, 1973.
Ennis, B. "The Place of Missing Films." *Motion Picture Magazine* 31, no. 5 (1926): 46–47.
Enticknap, Leo. *Moving Image Technology*. New York: Wallflower Press, 2005.
Epstein, Jean. "Langue D'Or." In *Jean Epstein: Critical Essays and New Translations*, eds. Sarah Keller and Jason N. Paul. Amsterdam: Amsterdam University Press, 2012.
Faure, Élie. "Cineplasticity." In *Film: An Anthology*, edited by Daniel Talbot, 5–16. Berkeley, CA: University of California Press, 1966.
Fay, Jennifer. *Inhospitable World: Cinema in the Time of the Anthropocene*. Oxford: Oxford University Press, 2018.
Feringa, Ben L. "In Control of Motion: From Molecular Switches to Molecular Motion." *Accounts of Chemical Research* 34, no. 6 (2001): 504–513.
Festa, Lynn. *Sentimental Figures of Empire in Eighteenth Century Britain and France*. Baltimore, MA: Johns Hopkins University Press, 2006.
Forbes, Esther. *Paul Revere and the World He Lived In*. Boston: Houghton Mifflin Harcourt, 1942.
Friedberg, Anne. *Window Shopping: Cinema and the Postmodern*. Berkeley: University of California Press, 1994.
Friedel, Robert. *Pioneer Plastic: The Making and Selling of Celluloid*. Madison: University of Wisconsin Press, 1983.
Furness, Dwight R. "Some Secrets of Screen Magic." In *Amateur Movie Makers* (January 15, 1927): 25–26.
Gardner, Jared. "What Blood Will Tell: Hereditary Determinism in *McTeague* and *Greed*." *Texas Studies in Literature and Language* 36, no. 1 (1994): 51–74.
Gaycken, Oliver. *Devices of Curiosity: Early Cinema and Popular Science*. Oxford: Oxford University Press, 2015.

Gerow, Aaron. "Early Cinema: Difference, Definition and Japanese Film Studies." In *The Japanese Cinema Book*, edited by Alastair Phillips and Hideaki Fujiki. London: Bloomsbury, 2020.

Gifford, Denis. *British Film Catalogue: Two Volume Set—The Fiction Film/The Non-Fiction Film*. London: Routledge, 2016.

Gomery, Douglas. *The Hollywood Studio System: A History*. London: Bloomsbury Academic, 2005.

Grieveson, Lee. *Cinema and the Wealth of Nations: Media, Capital, and the Liberal World System*. Berkeley: University of California Press, 2018.

Grosz, Elizabeth. *The Incorporeal: Ontology, Ethics and the Limits of Materialism*. New York: Columbia University Press, 2017.

Gunning, Tom. "'Primitive' Cinema: A Frame-up? or The Trick's on Us." *Cinema Journal* 28, no. 2 (1989): 3–12.

Gunning, Tom. "An Aesthetic of Astonishment: Early Film and the (In)credulous Spectator." In *Art and Text* 34 (Spring 1989): 76–95.

Gunning, Tom. "Tracing the Individual Body: Photography, Detectives, and Early Cinema." In *Cinema and the Invention of Modern Life*, edited by Lee Charney and Vanessa R. Schwarz. Berkeley, CA: University of California Press, 1996.

Gunning, Tom. "Modernity and Cinema: a Culture of Shocks and Flows." In *Cinema and Modernity*, edited by Murray Pomerance. New Jersey: Rutgers University Press, 2005a.

Gunning, Tom. "The Cinema of Attractions: Early Film, Its Spectators and the Avant-Garde." In *Cinema of Attractions Reloaded*, edited by Wanda Strauven. Amsterdam: Amsterdam University Press, 2005b.

Gunning, Tom. "Crazy Machines in the Garden of Forking Paths: Mischief Gags and the Origins of American Film Comedy." In *Classical Hollywood Comedy*, edited by Kristine Brunovska Karnick and Henry Jenkins. New York: Routledge, 2013a.

Gunning, Tom. "The Transforming Image." In *Pervasive Animation*, edited by Suzanne Buchan. London: Routledge, 2013b.

Gunning, Tom. "The Impossible Body of Early Film." *Corporeality in Early Cinema: Viscera, Skin, and Physical Form*, edited by Marina Dahlquist, Doron Galili, Jan Olsson, and Valentine Robert. Bloomington: Indiana University Press, 2018.

Haid, Jonathan. "The Raw Materials of Celluloid: Wartime Economy, Educational Animation, and Film's Plasticity." *Research in Film and History* 5 (2023): https://film-history.org/issues/text/raw-materials-celluloid-film

Hansen, Miriam. *Babel and Babylon*. Cambridge, MA: Harvard University Press, 2009.

Haraway, Donna. "Anthropocene, Capitalocene, Plantationocene, Chthulucene: Making Kin." *Environmental Humanities* 6, no. 1 (2015): 159–165.

Harman, Graham. *Object-Oriented Ontology: A New Theory of Everything*. London: Penguin UK, 2018.

Harris, Neil. *Humbug: The Art of P. T. Barnum*. Chicago: Chicago University Press, 1973.

Hasluck, Paul Nooncree. *The Book of Photography: Practical, Theoretic and Applied*. London: Cassell and Company Ltd., 1905.

Hepworth, Cecil M. *Animated Photography: The ABC of the Cinematograph*, 2nd Edition. Ludgate Hill: Hazel, Watson and Viney, 1900.

Hepworth, Cecil M. *Came the Dawn: Memories of a Film Pioneer*. London: Phoenix House, 1951.

Heinrich, Michael. *An Introduction to the Three Volumes of Karl Marx's Capital*. New York: NYU Press, 2012.

Hensley, Nathan K. and Philip Steer. "Signatures of the Carboniferus: The Literary Forms of Coal." In *Ecological Form: System and Aesthetics in the Age of Empire*, edited by Nathan K. Hensley and Philip Steer. New York: Fordham University Press, 2019.

Hickman, K. and D. Hyndman. "Automatic Silver Recovery from Hypo." In *Transactions of the Society of Motion Picture Engineers* 11, no. 32 (1927): pp. 699–706.

Jackson, Zakkiyah Iman. *Becoming Human: Matter and Meaning in an Anti-Black World*. New York: New York University Press, 2020.

Jacobson, Brian R. *Studios Before the System: Architecture, Technology, and the Emergence of Cinematic Space*. New York: Columbia University Press, 2015.

Jacobson, Brian R. *The Cinema of Extractions: Film Materials and Their Forms*. New York: Columbia University Press, 2025.

Jacobs, Lea. *The Decline of Sentiment: American Film in the 1920s*. Berkeley: University of California Press, 2009.

Jacoby, Sanford N. *Modern Manors: Welfare Capitalism Since the New Deal*. Princeton, NJ: Princeton University Press, 1998.

Jaikumar, Priya and Lee Grieveson, eds. "Film and Extraction." Special issue, *Media + Environment* 6, no. 1 (2024).

Jameson, Fredric. "The Shining." *Social Text* 4 (1981): 114–125.

Jameson, Fredric. *The Political Unconscious: Narrative as a Socially Symbolic Act*. New York: Routledge, 1983.

Jenkins, C. Francis. *Animated Pictures: An Exposition of the Historical Development of the Cinematograph*. Washington, DC: H. L. McQueen, 1898.

Kant, Immanuel. *Critique of Judgment*, translated by Werner S. Pluhar. Indianapolis: Hackett Press, 1987.

Keil, Charlie and Shelley Stamp. *American Cinema's Transitional Era: Audiences, Institutions, Practices*. Berkeley, CA: University of California Press, 2004.

Kendall, Tina. "Staying On or Getting Off (the Bus): Approaching Speed in Cinema and Media Studies." *Cinema Journal* 55, no. 2 (2016): 112–118.

Kessler, Frank. "Trick Films." In *Encyclopedia of Early Cinema*, edited by Richard Abel. New York: Routledge, 2005.

Kittler, Friedrich A. *Discourse Networks 1800/1900*, translated by Michael Metteer. Stanford, CA: Stanford University Press, 1985.
Kittler, Friedrich A. *Gramophone, Film, Typewriter*, translated by Geoffrey Winthrop-Young and Michael Wutz. Stanford, CA: Stanford University Press, 1999.
Knowles, Kim. *Experimental Film and Photochemical Practices*. New York: Spinger, 2020.
Koepnick, Lutz. *On Slowness: Toward an Aesthetic of the Contemporary*. New York: Columbia University Press, 2014.
Koszarski, Richard. *Von: The Life and Films of Erich von Stroheim*. New York: Limelight Press, 2001.
Landecker, Hannah. "Cellular Features: Microcinematography and Film Theory." *Critical Inquiry* 31, no. 4 (2005): 903–937.
Landecker, Hannah. "Microcinematography and the History of Science and Film." *Isis* 97, no. 1 (2006): 121–132.
Landecker, Hannah. "Creeping, Drinking, Dying: The Cinematic Portal and the Microscopic World of the Twentieth-Century Cell." *Science in Context* 24, no. 3 (2011): 381–416.
Latour, Bruno. *We Have Never Been Modern*. Cambridge, MA: Harvard University Press, 2012.
Latour, Bruno. *Reassembling the Social: An Introduction to Actor-Network Theory*. Oxford: Oxford University Press, 2007.
Léger, Fernand. "Ballet Mecanique." In *Functions of Painting*, edited by Edward F. Fry, translated by Alexandra Anderson. New York: Viking Press, 1973.
LeMenager, Stephanie. "The Aesthetics of Petroleum, after *Oil!*" *American Literary History* 24, no. 1 (2012): 59–86.
Levine, Caroline. *Form: Whole, Rhythm, Network*. Princeton: Princeton University Press, 2015.
Levinson, Marjorie. "What Is New Formalism?" *PMLA* 122, no. 2 (2007): 558–569.
Lippit, Akira Mizuta. *Atomic Light*. Minneapolis: University of Minnesota Press, 2005.
Lovejoy, Alice. "Celluloid Geopolitics: Film Stock and the War Economy, 1939–47." *Screen* 60, no. 2 (2019): 224–241.
Low, Rachel. *The History of the British Film 1906–1914*. London: Routledge, 1997.
Malabou, Catherine. *Plasticity at the Dusk of Writing: Dialectic, Destruction, Deconstruction*. New York: Columbia University Press, 2010.
Marx, Karl. *Capital: A Critique of Political Economy, Vol I*. London: Penguin, 2004.
Marzola, Luci. "Better Pictures through Chemistry: DuPont and the Fight for the Hollywood Film Stock Market." *The Velvet Light Trap* 76 (2015): 3–18.
Massumi, Brian. *Parables for the Virtual: Movement, Affect, Sensation*. Durham, NC: Duke University Press, 2021.
McKay, Herbert C. *Handbook of Motion Picture Photography*. London: Falk Publishing Company, 1927.

McKernan, Luke. *Charles Urban: Pioneering the Non-Fiction Film in Britain and America*. Exeter: University of Exeter Press, 2018.

Méliès, Georges. "Kinematographic Views: A Discussion by Georges Melies." In *Film and Attraction*, edited by Andrea Gaudreault, translated by Timothy Barnard. Springfield, IL: University of Illinois Press, 2011.

Meikle, Jeffrey L. *American Plastic: A Cultural History*. New Brunswick: Rutgers University Press, 1995.

Misek, Richard. *Chromatic Cinema: A History of Screen Colour*. Malden, MA: Wiley-Blackwell, 2010.

Mitchell, Pell. "Cameraman's Question Box." In *Exhibitor's Trade Review* 10, no. 21 (1921): 1479–1480.

Mitchell, W. J. T. "Image." In *Critical Terms for Media Studies*, edited by W. J. T. Mitchell and Mark B. N. Hansen. Chicago, IL: University of Chicago Press, 1985.

Moore, Jason W. "The Capitalocene, Part I: on the Nature and Origins of Our Ecological Crisis." *The Journal of Peasant Studies* 44, no. 3 (2017): 594–630.

Moretti, Franco. *Atlas of the European Novel: 1800–1900*. London: Verso, 1999.

Mulvey, Laura. *Fetishism and Curiosity*. Bloomington, IN: Indiana University Press, 2006.

Musser, Charles. *The Emergence of Cinema: The American Screen to 1907*. Berkeley: University of California Press, 1994.

Nelson, Anitra. "Marx's Theory of the Money Commodity." *History of Economics Review* 33, no. 1 (2001): 40–57.

Ngai, Sianne. *Our Aesthetic Categories: Zany, Cute, Interesting*. Cambridge, MA: Harvard University Press, 2012.

Ngai, Sianne. *Theory of the Gimmick: Aesthetic Judgment and Capitalist Form*. Cambridge, MA: Harvard University Press, 2020.

Noble, Peter. *Hollywood Scapegoat: The Biography of Erich von Stroheim*. London: Fortune Press, 1950.

Parikka, Jussi. *Digital Contagions: A Media Archaeology of Computer Viruses*. New York: Peter Lang, 2007.

Parikka, Jussi. "New Materialism as Media Theory: Medianatures and Dirty Matter." *Communication and Critical/Cultural Studies* 9, no. 1 (2012): 95–100.

Parikka, Jussi. *A Geology of Media*. Minneapolis: University of Minnesota Press, 2015.

Past, Elena. *Italian Ecocinema: Beyond the Human*. Bloomington: Indiana University Press, 2019.

Physioc, L. "Economy of Production." *American Cinematographer* 8, no. 12 (1928): 9–10.

Poli, Felix. "Microscope et Cinematographie." *Cine-Journal* 63 (November 1, 1909): 5–8.

Ramsaye, Terry. "The Romantic History of the Motion Picture." *Photoplay* 21, no. 5 (1922): 20–21.

Ramsaye, Terry. "Chemists Speed Printing Time of News Pictures in Colour." *Pathé Sun*, 5 April, 1930, 10.
Ray, Robert Beverley. *How a Film Theory Got Lost and Other Mysteries in Cultural Studies*. Bloomington: Indiana University Press, 2001.
Rosen, Miriam. "Méliès, Georges." In *World Film Directors: Volume I, 1890–1945*, edited by John Wakeman. New York: The H. W. Wilson Company, 1987.
Rossell, Deac. *Living Pictures*. Albany, NY: State University of New York Press, 1998.
Rossell, Deac. "Exploding Teeth, Unbreakable Sheets and Continuous Casting: Nitrocellulose from Gun-Cotton to Early Cinema." In *This Film Is Dangerous!*, edited by Roger Smither and Carol Surowiec. Brussels: International Federation of Film Archives [FIAF], 2003.
Schatz, Thomas. *The Genius of the System: Hollywood Filmmaking in the Studio Era*. New York: Henry Holt and Company, 2015.
Schelling, F. W. J. *Idealism and the Endgame of Theory: Three Essays*, edited by Thomas Pfau. Albany, NY: State University of New York Press, 2004.
Sedgwick, Eve Kosofsky. *Touching Feeling: Affect, Pedagogy, Performativity*. Durham, NC: Duke University Press, 2003.
Shaviro, Steven. *Post-Cinematic Affect*. Winchester, UK: Zero Books, 2010.
Sheppard, S. E. *Gelatin in Photography, Vol. 1*. New York: D. Van Nostrand Company, 1923.
Shirras, G. F. "Some Effects of the War on Gold and Silver." *Journal of the Royal Statistical Society* 83, no. 4 (1920): 572–627.
Shukin, Nicole. *Animal Capital: Rendering Life in Biopolitical Times*. Minneapolis: Minnesota University Press, 2009.
Siegert, Bernhard. *Cultural Techniques: Grids, Filters, Doors, and Other Articulations of the Real*. New York: Fordham University Press, 2015.
Silber, William L. *The Story of Silver: How the White Metal Shaped America and the Modern World*. New Jersey: Princeton University Press, 2019.
Skvirsky, Salomé Aguilera. *The Process Genre: Cinema and the Aesthetic of Labour*. Durham, NC: Duke University Press, 2020.
Slide, Anthony. *Nitrate Won't Wait: A History of Film Preservation in the United States*. Jefferson, NC: McFarland, 2013.
Smith, Steven B. *Modernity and Its Discontents: Making and Unmaking the Bourgeois from Machiavelli to Bellow*. New Haven, CT: Yale University Press, 2016.
Smither, Roger B. N. *This Film Is Dangerous: A Celebration of Nitrate Film*. Brussels: Federation Internationale des Archives du Film (FIAF), 2002.
Solomon, Matthew. *Disappearing Tricks: Silent Film, Houdini, and the New Magic of the Twentieth Century*. Chicago: University of Illinois Press, 2010.
Szczepaniak-Gillece, Jocelyn and Stephen Groening. "Afterword: Objects in the Theater." *Film History* 28, no. 3 (2016): 139–142.
Szendy, Peter. *Apocalypse-Cinema: 2012 and Other Ends of the World*. New York: Fordham University Press, 2015.

Talbot, Frederick A. *Moving Pictures: How They Are Made and Worked*. London: William Heinemann, 1914.
Thompson, Kristen and David Bordwell, *Film History: An Introduction*. New York: McGraw-Hill Education, 2019.
Turvey, Malcolm. "Vertov: Between the Organism and the Machine." *October* 121 (2007): 5–18.
Vaughan, Hunter. "500,000 Kilowatts of Stardust." *Sustainable Media*, edited by Janet Walker and Nicole Starosielski. New York, NY: Routledge, 2016.
Vaughan, Hunter. *Hollywood's Dirtiest Secret: The Hidden Environmental Costs of the Movies*. New York: Columbia University Press, 2019.
von Stackelberg, Emmet. "'The Fatal Blemish': Purity, Consistency, and Chemical Engineers at the Origin of a New Visual Order, 1890–1930." *Enterprise and Society* (2024): 1–26.
Walker, Janet and Nicole Starosielski, eds. *Sustainable Media*. New York, NY: Routledge 2016.
Wasko, Janet. *Movies and Money: Financing the American Film Industry*. Stamford, CT: ABLEX Publishing Corporation, 1982.
Wees, Beth Carver and Medill Higgins Harvey. *Early American Silver in The Metropolitan Museum of Art*. New York, NY: Metropolitan Museum of Art, 2013.
Whissel, Kristin. *Spectacular Visual Effects: CGI and Contemporary Cinema*. Durham, NC: Duke University Press, 2014.
Williamson, Colin. *Hidden in Plain Sight: An Archaeology of Magic and the Cinema*. New Brunswick, NJ: Rutgers University Press, 2015.
Wilson, Sheena, Imre Szeman, and Adam Carlson. "On Petrocultures: Or, Why We Need to Understand Oil to Understand Everything Else." In *Petrocultures: Oil, Politics, Culture*, edited by Sheena Wilson, Adam Carlson, and Imre Szeman. Montreal: McGill-Queen's Press-MQUP.
Winton, R. W. "Why Films Go Wrong." *Movie Makers*, May 1929, 287–289.
Wolfe, Cary. *What is Posthumanism?* Minneapolis: University of Minnesota Press, 2010.
Wollen, Peter. "Speed and the Cinema." *New Left Review* 16 (2002): 105.
Worden, Edward Chauncey. *Nitrocellulose Industry: A Compendium of the History, Chemistry, Manufacture, Commercial Application and Analysis of Nitrates, Acetates and Xanthates of Cellulose as Applied to the Peaceful Arts, with a Chapter on Gun Cotton, Smokeless Powder and Explosive Cellulose Nitrates, vol. II*. New York, NY: D. van Nostrand Company, 1911.
Young, Paul. "Media on Display: A Telegraphic History of Early American Cinema." In *New Media: 1740–1915*, edited by Lisa Gitelman and Geoffrey B. Pingree. Cambridge, MA: MIT Press, 2003.
Yumibe, Joshua. *Moving Color: Early Film, Mass Culture, Modernism*. New Brunswick, NJ: Rutgers University Press, 2012.
Zimmermann, Patricia. *Reel Families: A Social History of Amateur Film*. Bloomington: Indiana University Press, 1995.

Index

A Movie Trip Through Filmland, 6, 78–80
Adorno, Theodor, 14, 73, 89, 103
aesthetics, 1, 3–6, 10–14, 16–17, 27, 43, 51, 69–73, 84–6, 89–90, 97–101
Althusser, Louis, 11–12
Anthropocene, 4, 6
Arabindan-Kesson, Anna, 29–30
Avengers, The, 101

bacteria, 1, 4, 8–9, 15–16, 49–52, 55–7
Bauman, Zygmunt, 29
Ball, Philip, 100
Brown, William, 34, 81
Benjamin, Walter, 14, 58, 103
Bennett, Jane, 3, 10, 77
Boetzkes, Amanda, 8
Bordwell, David, 84, 89, 92, 101–2
Bourne franchise, 101
Bozak, Nadia, 99
Bruno, Giuliana, 6, 14, 28
Buell, Frederick, 8

Cahill, James Leo, 6, 14
Came the Dawn, 47, 49, 65
capitalism, 2, 8, 10, 77, 97, 98

Carpenter-Goldman Laboratories, 86
celluloid, 1, 2, 4, 5, 6, 9, 11, 13, 14–15, 24–44, 50, 76, 85, 97–9
Celluloid Manufacturing Co., 27
classical Hollywood cinema, 4, 16, 71, 73, 84, 90
Clown and Policeman, 31, 36–7, 40–1
Comandon, Jean, 50, 52, 59–61, 63–5, 67
Crary, Jonathan, 31, 47
Corwin, Sharon, 77
Cubitt, Sean, 3

Daston, Lorraine, 58,
Dickson, Antonia, 25, 52,
Dickson, W. K. L., 25,
Doane, Mary Ann, 38, 46, 81
Dootson, Kirsty, 58

early cinema, 1–3, 5, 9, 13, 15, 17, 27, 31, 36, 47, 51, 73, 79, 97
Eastman, George, 82
Eastman Kodak, 2, 52, 54, 56, 57, 61, 62, 77, 82, 86–7, 98
eco-materialism, 1, 2–3, 6, 10, 25, 27, 42–3, 44, 72, 97
Ellis, Franklin, 76, 94, 106

Enticknap, Leo, 33
Epstein, Jean, 87–9
Explosion of a Motor Car, 30, 36, 37
extraction, 2, 7, 11, 18, 44, 54, 74, 81, 94

Fay, Jennifer, 6
Festa, Lynn, 4, 74
Fleming, David, 34
form, 3–8, 10, 12, 13, 14, 16, 25, 27, 29, 33, 34–5, 42, 71–2, 90, 99, 101

Galison, Peter, 58
Gaycken, Oliver, 59
gelatin, 1, 2, 4, 5, 6, 9, 10, 11, 13, 15–16, 30, 49–68, 75, 98, 99, 100
Gelatin in Photography, 53, 55
German media theory, 2, 5
Greed, 69, 85–6
Gunning, Tom, 31, 34, 40, 41

Harris, Neil, 79
Hepworth, Cecil M., 9, 15, 24–47, 49–50, 65
Hollywood, 2, 4, 5, 13, 16, 69–73, 75, 83–9, 92, 96, 97, 99
Horkheimer, Max, 73, 89

image, 5–6, 9, 14–15, 25–6, 30–43, 58–9, 61–5, 75, 77, 79, 80, 96, 97

Jackson, Zakiyyah Iman, 29, 42
Jacobson, Brian, 6, 7
Jameson, Fredric, 12

Kant, Immanuel, 57
Keaton, Buster, 6
Kracauer, Siegfried, 14, 32
Koepnick, Lutz, 101
Kodak Park, 77, 81–2

"Langue D'Or," 87–9
Latour, Bruno, 13, 72, 91–2
Legér, Fernand, 87–8, 109
LeMenager, Stephanie, 8
Lippit, Akira, 34–5
lithium, 17, 100
Lovejoy, Alice, 11, 105, 109

magic, 5, 14, 16, 24, 28, 31, 32, 35, 46, 70–92, 94, 97, 99
Malabou, Catherine, 29, 35, 44
Marx, Karl, 24, 30–1, 37, 53, 99
material, 2, 4–6, 8, 10–17, 19–20, 25–33, 35, 42–3, 50–5, 57–9, 64–5, 71–4, 76, 79–80, 83–4, 87, 89–90, 92, 97, 99–100
Mattison, Frank, 82
Melies, Georges, 31–2, 35, 46
Meikle, Jeffrey, 26, 28,
Mitchell, W. J. T., 5

natural history, 6, 14
Ngai, Sianne, 5, 25, 70, 72

Past, Elena, 6–7, 110
Parikka, Jussi, 3, 97
Pittman Act, 82
plasticity, 1, 4, 8–9, 11, 24–6, 28–9, 33–6, 39, 42, 52

Ray, Robert, 73
representation, 2, 7, 10, 19, 33, 72, 79

sentimental commodity, 4, 9, 16, 72, 74–5, 81, 90

Shukin, Nicole, 53
silver, 1, 2, 4, 5, 6, 9, 10, 11, 13, 14, 16, 43, 44, 50, 51, 54, 55, 69–92, 94, 96, 98–9, 100
Silver Comes Through, 70
Silver King, The, 70

Silver Reclamation, 84–5
Silver Treasure, 70

TikTok, 99

Ultramicroscope Time-Lapse of Syphilis Parasite, 50

Solomon, Matthew, 73
Spirochaeta Pallida, 16, 59, 60, 63–5
Steer, Philip, 8
Szendy, Peter, 34

technology, 1, 5–7, 11, 17, 32, 39, 43, 51, 57–8, 64–5, 72, 79, 81, 83, 86–7, 89, 97, 99, 101

Thalberg, Irving, 69
Transformers, 101
trick film, 4, 7, 9, 11, 15, 27, 30–1, 34–7, 40–1, 97, 99

Vaughan, Hunter, 3, 19, 99
Vertov, Dziga, 58
von Stroheim, Erich, 69–70, 85–6

Weingarten, Alfred, 86–7
World War I, 13, 16, 70–1, 74, 82
Wollen, Peter, 101

Young, Paul, 79, 94

Zimmermann, Patricia, 83

EU representative:
Easy Access System Europe
Mustamäe tee 50, 10621 Tallinn, Estonia
Gpsr.requests@easproject.com

www.ingramcontent.com/pod-product-compliance
Lightning Source LLC
Chambersburg PA
CBHW051132160426
43195CB00014B/2441